D1708931

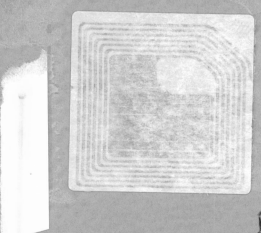

A Book Based on Guillermo Kuitca

A Book Based on

Guillermo Kuitca

Contemporary Art Foundation Amsterdam

Guillermo Kuitca Exhibition
IVAM Centre del Carme, Valencia
Museo de Monterrey, Monterrey
Museo Rufino Tamayo – Instituto
Nacional de Bellas Artes, Mexico City
Center for the Fine Arts, Miami
Musée National d'Art Moderne,
Centre G. Pompidou, Paris

Curators
Eduardo Lipschutz-Villa
Vicente Todolí

Coordination
Nuria Enguita

We would like to acknowledge the
support given to us by:

Fernando Bustillo
Bernadette Bout
Barbara Farber
Jorge Helft
Arthur Hulst
Louis Grachos
Cristina Galvez Guzzy
Rolinka Kattouw
Dirk Kleiman
Claudio Gonzales Landa
Jean de Loisy
Margreet Monhemius
Jorge García Murillo
Annina Nosei
Mariana Oberzstern
Alan Pauls
Jill Rowe
Gian Enzo Sperone
Ranti Tjan
Gandee Vaikunthavasan
Angela Westwater

And the Buenos Aires crew:
Hugo Aizemberg
Ernesto Ballesteros
Alfredo Londaibere
Jorge Miño
Pablo Siquier

With special thanks to:
Eduardo Alvarez
Sonia Becce
Nuria Enguita

Some of the creative stories authored
by Martin Rejtman are accounts of
stories related to Rejtman by the artist
Guillermo Kuitca. Others are based on
the author's own experiences; still
others are intended to serve as
vignettes of Kuitca's life. The publisher
wishes to acknowledge the
graciousness of all persons who have
lent their names and likenesses to
these stories.

ISBN 90-73170-03-6

Printed in Holland

Contents

Foreword

Guillermo Kuitca, born in Buenos Aires in 1961, has consolidated his presence in major contemporary art centers in Europe and the Americas during recent years. The exhibition which the IVAM initiated includes a wide-ranging selection from the various series he has produced in the last decade, allowing a thorough study of the evolution of his artistic language. The relationship of Kuitca's work to theatre and literature is a basic factor which can be seen in the influence of scenographic ideas and in the poetic association of visual and literary forms of expression. The everyday items which stand out in his last few series emphasize the clarification of a system of signs linking personal space with external geography. Surprise at the intimate landscape within leads the gaze towards the space outside, represented through the abstraction of maps and charts.

Kuitca is an outstanding example of breaching boundaries. Cultures and disciplines, systems of signs and languages are transformed and presented anew from a viewpoint which is not without a dramatic element. Sentimental topography is superimposed on the anonymity of travel. Viewing Kuitca's work means exploring the tension between a hermetic world and a world without frontiers.

Valencia 1993
Carmen Alborch
Executive Director of the IVAM

Foreword

Arriving in Buenos Aires I detected the smell of airplane fuel hanging in the air. This familiar smell elicited a rush of childhood memories: Sleepless nights before my departure, my mind whirring with anticipation and expectation, imagining what I might experience in the true European capital of South America. Ever still, when I think of Buenos Aires I can smell the *nafta* that invades one's senses upon arrival, an odor somewhat becoming to this city teaming with European immigrants who typify the common *porteno* or resident of this oddly Parisianesque city.

Stepping out of the airplane I was confronted by a sense of change. Leaflets for incoming duty free shopping were handed to me, as though outgoing duty free had been deemed insufficient. The customs officer, a lady dedicated to the task of interrogating hosts of travel-weary passengers on a daily basis, asked what my line of work was and what business I had in Buenos Aires. When I told her that I'd come to visit Argentinean artists, I sensed the flowering of a smile. Ah yes, she said, waving me through, We have many of them and they make such beautiful things. I left customs and walked into the central airport terminal where I was accosted by a huge sign hanging just in front of the exit: Last Chance Duty Free Shop. After years of austerity, shopping has become a national pastime in a city long-since dominated by psychoanalysts and football fanatics.

When I first met Guillermo Kuitca I was pleased to be able to identify with his background: Of European descent, born and raised in South America, possessing a purely Latin soul, believing that he is one hundred percent South American despite ancestral immigration. Kuitca's work captures moments of knowledge, vestiges of history, memories of feelings so exquisitely private that viewers are led to feel like intruders. It's a long time since I've been so thoroughly absorbed by the privateness of painting.

This book is a journey into the life and work of Guillermo Kuitca, at once illuminated by the reproduction of his work, by the stories related by the artist and written by Martin Rejtman, and by the thoughtful and provocative essays authored by Marcelo E. Pacheco and Jerry Saltz. It is hoped that this book will serve to place the work of this virile young artist in context vis-à-vis Buenos Aires and the world's capitals.

I once asked Kuitca whether he would consider moving from Buenos Aires and before I finished posing the question I was answering it myself. Kuitca embodies the spirit of Buenos Aires. In order to survive he needs the city with all its virtues and all its problems, in good times and in bad times. Attempting to impose some sense of order on the world, organizing it into maps, grids and genealogical charts, is Kuitca's way of liberating himself from the enthralling chaos that presides over the world outside his studio.

8

I am grateful to the authors who contributed their work and ideas to this publication and who, together with me, share a tremendous love for Guillermo Kuitca's work. Since its inception four years ago, this book has undergone its own process of discovery and change, coinciding as it has with the evolution of an artist whose work is continually surprising and fresh. It has been a unique process, the spirit of which is bound between these two covers. I am convinced that Kuitca's work will achieve heights as yet unimaginable. Here is an artist who radiates a sense of history in the making. I am especially grateful to Guillermo for giving me the opportunity to realize my vision for this book. I am one of many affected by the magic of Kuitca.

I wish to express my gratitude to Angela Westwater who, with the support of her staff at the Sperone Westwater Gallery, has been instrumental in the creation of this book. I also wish to thank those whose likenesses can be found in the portrayals crafted by Martin Rejtman; your graciousness on behalf of Guillermo Kuitca is greatly appreciated.

This book was conceived on the occasion of the exhibition featuring Guillermo Kuitca at the Instituto Valenciano de Arte Moderno (IVAM) in Valencia. I want to thank both Carmen Alborch and Vicente Todolí who, over the past several years, supported the dream of this publication and who allowed me to co-curate the exhibition with Vicente Todolí.

I shall continue to be reminded of people who supported me in this endeavor. Changes occur, new directions are taken, but feelings of gratitude remain the same.

Eduardo Lipschutz-Villa
Amsterdam 1993

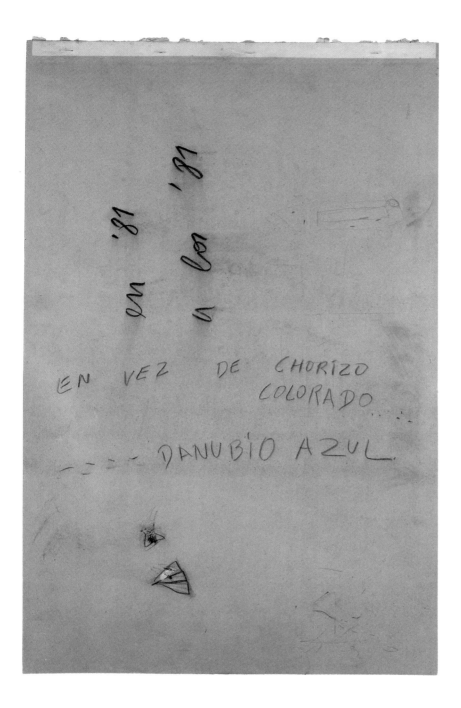

En vez de chorizo colorado
Danubio azul, 1981
Charcoal on paper
71 x 45 cm
Collection of the artist

Untitled, 1989
Offset
24.8 x 39.8 cm
Collection of the artist

Untitled, 1989
Offset
24.8 x 39.8 cm
Collection of the artist

12

Untitled, 1982
Acrylic on canvas
35.2 x 23.8 cm
Collection of the artist

Untitled, 1982
Watercolor on paper
35.2 x 23.8 cm
Collection of the artist

Untitled, 1982
Watercolor on paper
35.2 x 23.8 cm
Collection of the artist

Untitled, 1982
Watercolor on paper
35.2 x 23.8 cm
Collection of the artist

16

Antiedipo, 1982
Charcoal on paper
23 x 34 cm
Collection of the artist

Martin Rejtman

Thirty-four Stories

Translated by Edward Shaw

The Child Painter

Just before my ninth birthday, my parents took me to see a child artist who was a little older than me. The boy was having a show in a gallery, and when we got there he was sitting by himself in the middle of the exhibit space. My dad and the owner of the gallery introduced me to the artist and we chatted for a while; he seemed like a very formal child. He was two years older than me, and at one point he placed his arm over my shoulder and led me through the exhibit, showing me his paintings.

There were landscapes, rowboats, ships; it was one of the most moving moments I can remember. I never heard anything more about this child artist. I'd give anything today to know what became of him.

The years rolled by. Every day I felt more sure that what I really wanted was to be a painter. At twelve I already considered myself a professional, and together with Ahuva, my teacher, and my parents, I believed the moment had arrived to go out and find a gallery.

The first step was to go to Gradiva, a gallery that was in a basement with stuccoed walls on San Martín Street. I went with my father and we were received by the lady who owned the gallery. I didn't speak and my daddy said, 'We've come to propose that you do a show of his work.'

'I imagine as much,' the lady at Gradiva answered. 'Artists never bring their children here.'

In spite of everything, we managed to convince the woman to meet us at our home the following Monday, very late at night.

We had just the weekend to arrange everything, and there was a lot to be done. Ahuva spent all Saturday and Sunday ironing and preparing folders to put everything in. The work was somewhat wrinkled since I kept everything rolled up.

On Monday night, my father, my mother, my sister and I were all sitting on the big sofa in our living room. Ahuva was smoking like crazy. And there was also this lady looking at my pictures. When she was finished, my sister and I went to bed because we had to go to school in the morning.

The school bus brought me home at lunchtime and as soon as I sat down at the table, my father told me that the lady from Gradiva had given the work her OK, but in order to protect me she had decided not to have an exhibition, and she emphatically recommended that I not exhibit anywhere else either.

In a rage I went to see her in her basement on San Martín Street and told her that she really disgusted me and that what she had said was the biggest crock of shit in the world. The woman, without even getting ruffled, answered, 'A very young painter, more or less your age, exhibited at the Biennial of São Paulo and when he went to cross the street he was run over by a car. I don't want to do you any harm.'

I had the impression that that artist must have been the same child painter that I had seen several years before in that gallery, my real mentor. When I finally held my first show a couple of months later, a new child artist came to the gallery, this time to see my work. I tried to reproduce that previous moment, putting my arm over his shoulder, leading him through the exhibit, showing him my paintings one by one.

Finta's Hat

I went to spend the weekend in Miramar just two days before traveling to New York. I was spread out on the sand sunbathing when a child about six, strolling by hand in hand with his grandfather, stopped in front of me.

'Mister,' he said to me.

At first I thought he was talking to someone else. I am not used to anyone saying Mister to me, but there wasn't anyone else on that stretch of beach.

'Mister,' he said again to me. 'Can I count the toes on your feet?'

I told him he could and he counted to ten. His grandfather seemed a bit ill at ease. It was the middle of January, the dead of summer, and I was spending my last days with my family in Argentina at the beach.

The heat when I got back to Buenos Aires was unbearable. I had just enough time to go home, change suitcases and continue on to the airport.

*   *   *

The opening of Guillermo's show at Annina's was the following day, and Finita couldn't find the $ 800 top hat that she had bought at Comme des Garçons especially for the event.

Finita was desperate. She searched every corner of the gallery, emptying all the drawers. She turned all the paintings in the storage room around, but the hat did not appear. She suddenly remembered that at one point during the evening she had seen Georges Helft joking and laughing with the hat as if he were a master of ceremonies. She decided to call him on the phone to see if he might have a lead. It was 4:00 a.m.

'I am calling you so late because I know that you are leaving New York tomorrow.'

'Look, I don't have the slightest idea where your fancy hat can be,'
Helft answered.

As Finita had bought the hat with her American Express card, she decided to file a claim. The form suggested three possibilities:

a it fell off and was broken;

b it was stolen;

c mysterious disappearance.

Finita didn't hesitate. She put a cross next to 'mysterious disappearance' with the following explanation:

We went to this party with the hat and I left the hat in the cloakroom, and when I went to get it, the hat wasn't there anymore.

In a few days American Express sent her the $ 800, Finita is still waiting for the mysterious reappearance of her top hat.

Twist and Shout

That afternoon we went to have tea at Finita's.

Finita brought two bottles of Perrier to the table.

'They're poisoned,' I told her. The day before it had been announced that Perrier mineral water contained some kind of toxic substance that was harmful to one's health. Everyone was talking about it; it was all over the newspapers and on television.

'Not these,' Finita declared. 'The poisoned bottles are the ones that have a twist of lime or orange.'

We drank three bottles of Perrier between the four of us.

The next day I found out that all of Perrier's production, twists included, was being withdrawn from restaurants, supermarkets, shops and cafes throughout the United States.

Terrified, I decided to call the Perrier hot line, 1-800-PERRIER. I told them that I had drank more than a liter of Perrier and I asked if I should check myself into a hospital. The young woman who assisted me didn't seem to know much about the matter and had to consult someone else.

'What symptoms do you have?' she asked me when she got back on the hot line.

'Right now, none,' I responded.

'In that case don't worry. The quantity of benzene that there is in a liter of Perrier cannot have harmed you.'

Later I learned that Finita was buying cases of Perrier in large lots, and at the rear of her loft she had a small room where she stored hundreds and hundreds of liters of the poisoned French mineral water.

Anticipation

Several days after the catastrophe at Gradiva, Guillermo's mom took him to a show of Perla Fainstein's, who happened to be her dentist at the time. Perla Fainstein was totally wacky; she was very fat, an old maid, and her office overlooked a construction site. She claimed the workers stared at her. She had even spoken to the foreman to accuse some of them.

Perla Fainstein painted cats and the room where she was exhibiting was over a drug store. After looking at the paintings, Guillermo's mom told Perla what had happened when they had gone to look for a gallery.

'Why don't you go see the Fanos?' Perla suggested.

Paulette Fano was a remarkably tall and ugly woman, with all her teeth sticking out, and she and her husband were blessed with a sophistication and refinement far beyond the ordinary. Their gallery was called Lirolay. It was a unique place in the history of Argentinean art because it was open to everyone. The rooms could be rented for a fair price and could be paid with the commissions on the first sales.

Paulette and her husband had the same reservations as the woman at Gradiva and they said that they didn't want to do Guillermo any harm. Once again he was very upset, and finally they gave him a show on 16 September. Perla Fainstein's suggestion had paid off.

Guillermo's father decided to finance the show on the condition that Guillermo didn't skip going to the 'Y' anymore, where he went to exercise. They had discovered that he played hooky because the clothes in his bag were always clean. Guillermo would go to the Galería del Este, a bohemian shopping arcade where he had befriended a lady who sold arty posters and who let him sit on her styrofoam chairs.

The day of the show, 16 September, coincided with Rosh Hashana and that caused a lot of problems because people had to combine their family dinners with the opening. Both were at the same hour.

Guillermo's mother had always been very respectful of these dates and her family celebrated them, but this year she was totally secular.

'What does Rosh Hashana matter to us,' she said.

Guillermo had decided not to hang any of his old work and prepared a completely new series. Most of the titles of the paintings were taken from a Carly Simon LP, songs like 'Share the end' and 'Anticipation;'. other titles were taken from prayers. All the works were signed in the lower right-hand corner.

During the show, Guillermo went to the gallery everyday. There was a show of work by Margarita Galetar in the room next to his. Margarita Galetar was a typical nutty broad, besides being Liliana Porter's mother, and she had done a series of drawings for UNICEF. The gallery was selling the cards which reproduced the works she was showing.

In those days the atmosphere at Lirolay was very special. It was the time of the guerrilla group Montoneros, and men with beards and women who smoked incessantly turned up at the gallery. Guillermo joined in their conversations and discussions; among other things they expounded on the bourgeois issue of an artist's need to show in galleries.

The second day Ruth Benzacar came; at the end of the first week Blackie called to invite Guillermo to appear on her TV program. But he didn't go because he was supposed to bring the pictures to the studio and he refused to take them out of the gallery. *La Opinión,* the daily newspaper, published a review because an uncle of Guillermo's knew Jacobo Timmerman.

From a financial point of view the show was also a success; so much so that six of the eleven pictures were sold. Guillermo says that his father took charge of all that, and that he never saw a single penny out of the sales.

According to Jaime Kuitca, he used the money from the sale of the six works by his son to finance a catalogue, pay two weeks' rent for the exhibition space, hire a catering service for the opening, a cleaning lady and a photographer. All the sales were made to relatives and friends, with the exception of one; and Guillermo's family never heard anything more about that particular picture or the unknown buyer again.

Opening Night

For the inauguration of his first show in Rio, Guillermo and Sonia thought of a lot of different ways to dress, but the ones that got the most votes were a nun's habit for her and a bullfighter's outfit or a priest's robes for him.

As there are no bullfights in Brazil, the first thing they did was to look for 'religious articles' in the yellow pages. Guillermo and Sonia didn't speak a word of Portuguese and they didn't know how to say nun, so they added a Portuguese flavor to the Spanish word *monja*. Their version was *monsha*. The shop girls showed them everything from pieces of the human body and paraphernalia for Carnival to objects to be offered to Iemanjá.

They spent several days doing this, lost and without direction, until Miguel Harte gave them the magic word: *freira*. Armed with the Portuguese word for nun, they began to visit convents. Guillermo was dressed in Bermudas and a sleeveless t-shirt and Sonia was wearing an imitation leopard-skin mini. They would say they were part of a theatrical troupe and that they were looking for religious outfits to play *Agnes of God* in Buenos Aires.

As was to be expected, the tour of convents was a failure; not a single nun wanted to sell her habit. But at the end of the day they stumbled upon a very austere boutique in the heart of downtown Rio, where the woman who assisted them treated them like charlatans, informing them that habits for priests or nuns were not made in Brazil but were imported from Argentina. To emphasize her point, she read them her price list; everything was outrageously expensive and, in any case, there were no priest's outfits left in stock. So, to get out of their predicament, it was decided that it would be Guillermo who would dress as a nun. Unfortunately the only thing the woman could offer them was a sort of mountaineer's headgear made of white linen and that tied in the front; it was in fact the little white toga through which nuns stick their heads.

Sonia decided that Guillermo had to appear as someone else on the night of the inauguration; that he would speak only in Spanish, stay in a corner, have flecks of gray hair, wear dark glasses and only drink mineral water. A real tough guy.

They spent another day looking for the right product to dye his hair gray around the edges. They finally found it at a hairdresser's at Rio Sul. They were so nervous that both of them hid in the men's room at the shopping center and Sonia sprayed the liquid on his head right there. They had gotten it just in time; that evening was the opening night.

Illegal Weapons

One night in New York, Guillermo, Nora, Lisa and I decided to get together to go to discotheques. We agreed to meet at a modern Israeli bar called 'Lox Around the Clock;' I think it was open all night long. We liked the place because it was pretty corny and could perfectly well have been in Buenos Aires. During the three quarters of an hour we were there we never stopped putting coins in the juke box waiting to hear the songs that we had programmed, but there must have been a glitch in the system, because we didn't get to listen to any of those songs.

When we left the bar we walked a few blocks. We were getting closer and closer to the river. It was a neglected area, mostly uninhabited, with enormous industrial warehouses. On reaching the discotheque some friends who had been living in New York for several years had recommended, we saw a very large sign on the doorway, written by hand on white paper, which said: '*All illegal weapons will be taken away from you.*' Since none of the four of us had any, we kept on going; at the end of the same street there was another discotheque where only blacks were going in. We liked the place and after checking our coats, they frisked us to see if we were carrying any kind of *illegal weapon*.

The discotheque was called Kilimanjaro. The whole lower part was an immense warehouse, with an atmosphere similar to that of the dance halls in poor districts on the outskirts of Buenos Aires, but this place was a cut above them. Everyone was very well dressed; they played African music and the beat immediately set us moving to the rhythm. After a while the pace became monotonous and we decided to check out the other floor. Upstairs there was another dance floor and another bar, much smaller, where they were playing black music (rap, disco, soul, etc.) and there were just a few people. We danced there, too, until they put on a slow tune and Lisa tried to dance with me. In the beginning I refused, but she was so insistent that I had to accept. Right away I proved I was incapable of following the rhythm, stepping on her foot several times. Lisa got mad (by now I had discovered she was pretty temperamental).

'Agh. What did you do while the others were dancing the slow numbers?' She asked me in Spanish with a very peculiar accent and with her characteristic nasal voice. The question was so vague that I couldn't figure out how to answer it. Fortunately they played a bouncy rap right then and I put some break dance steps into practice that I had learned from a TV program a few years ago.

We soon got tired and left. Someone suggested we go to Mars, which was quite nearby, also in that same neighborhood by the river. No one was very sure where it was; the taxi driver wasn't either.

'MARS!' Lisa said to him, impatiently. 'M-A-R-S!' She ended up spelling it out for him.

We saw some kids go by who'd done their hair up with gel, had ponytails and wore their jackets with the sleeves rolled up, and the driver rolled down his window to ask them. One of them pointed to the sky and the other made a signal indicating that we should keep going straight down the same street. Luckily the taxi driver paid attention to the second kid and kept going straight ahead. Somehow it didn't seem right that these kids knew Mars.

We recognized where it was because there were a lot of kids in the doorway, all with gel, ponytails and rolled-up sleeves. They were waiting to be picked out by the doorman in order to get in. We stopped at the entrance and while we were arguing about whether we wanted to be picked out or not, the doorman signaled to us and we marched in. We looked around the ground floor: Everyone was dancing, there were colored lights and giant dolls wrapped in silver foil; it looked like the Parakultural, with a bit more emphasis on the production. We decided to go, and while we were discussing what to do with the rest of our night, we stopped outside of Mars again, among the people waiting to get in. The doorman picked us out again, and in that moment he must have realized that we were already inside because, in a state of confusion, he began looking all over the place. When he looked at us again, the four of us refused at the same time with a nod of the head and we moved on.

We didn't know what to do for the rest of the night. Someone suggested we go to MK or, as it was Friday, to the Lambada Nights at Palladium, but coming from South America, neither of the two options seemed to be worth the effort.

So we decided to go to an old American-style coffee shop that was nearby and had a typically '50s look, like you see in music videos, where they now served nouvelle cuisine and people went before or after going to discotheques.

'How disgusting,' Guillermo said.

'Agh! What did you expect?' Lisa responded.

'Conchudos,' I echoed in Spanish.

'What?' Nora and Lisa asked simultaneously. I should point out that Lisa is American; Nora isn't, but she has been living in the States for a number of years now and had lost contact a bit with our country.

'Conchudos,' Guillermo repeated.

'Shell people,' I translated literally.

'People of the shells,' Lisa reinterpreted even more literally in Spanish.

'Yes,' Guillermo answered in order to put an end to it all, and the four of us went into the coffee shop, where they all ordered American coffee and I asked for herbal tea.

Annina vs Carpio

Jacobo Carpio called Guillermo on the telephone to tell him that he wanted to print 200 posters to take with him to New York as a present for Guillermo's show at Annina's. Guillermo warned him not to bring them to the United States or he would get himself into trouble.

But Carpio managed to get to New York with the posters anyway. He had reproduced a painting of Guillermo's that wasn't in the exhibit, but which he had for sale in Costa Rica. It was on a black background, you could barely read the name Guillermo Kuitca, and in enormous white letters that seemed like an attempt to imitate the typical typography of the Bauhaus, but actually was a modern Central American font, it read: ANNINA NOSEI GALLERY, and below that, COURTESY JACOBO CARPIO, followed by the address of his gallery in Costa Rica.

Guillermo said that he decided immediately to save Carpio and he hid all the posters in the apartment that Finita had in Soho, so that Annina would never see them. When Carpio went back to Costa Rica, he took all the posters with him.

But Annina ended up finding out about the whole thing anyway. Since Carpio didn't know what to do with his posters, it seems he decided to use them to wallpaper the city of San Jose, to do a bit of self-promotion. A friend of Annina, who was vacationing there, noticed them and phoned New York to congratulate her, delighted to discover that she was going to open a gallery in the Caribbean.

Months later, at the Chicago Art Fair, a dark man walked up to Annina, smiling, and asked her: 'Do you know who I am?'

'No, I don't know who you are,' Annina responded.

'You don't know who I am?'

'No, I don't have the slightest idea who you are.'

'So you don't know who I am?'

'No! No, I don't know who you are,' Annina answered impatiently.

'Well, I am Jacobo Carpio.'

Annina was speechless. Finally they ended up chatting and she decided to forget the episode. But since Carpio wouldn't go away, Annina had to say to him, 'Look, I'll forgive you, but if you don't get out of here I am going to forget that I forgave you and I am going to have to sue you right now.'

Last week I ran into Carpio in an Italian restaurant in Buenos Aires; when we greeted each other I asked him if he had had any problems with the law recently.

Madrid Sucks

A fire that forced revelers to evacuate a Madrid disco left the cloakroom attend-ant with 300 portable telephones. *After two weeks, only two-thirds had been reclaimed. Police found the rest were fakes.*
The Guardian, 17 *January* 1992

I called Lisa, the same American girl of the discotheques in New York, from Barajas Airport. She had invited me to spend a few days at her home. I said, 'I'm in Madrid.'

She replied, 'Grab a taxi; it's too much of a drag to explain the buses. Any-way it's not expensive. It's about a thousand.'

I didn't have much money then and the taxi that I grabbed came out closer to two thousand, while the bus would have cost two hundred pesetas.

I got to her home and Lisa opened the door. She was in a bathrobe and looked completely pale.

'Agh. I've been vomiting all night,' she declared, with her peculiar accent and characteristic nasal voice.

I was holding my suitcase, which was heavy, and still standing outside the door. So I walked in.

'I am going to the bathroom,' Lisa said, holding her stomach, and she disap-peared down a hallway. She still hadn't even said hello.

'Hello,' I heard someone else saying. It was another girl in a bathrobe, this time a Spaniard, who crossed the living room as pale as a ghost. 'We didn't sleep much last night.'

Like Lisa, she disappeared down the same hallway. I heard her banging on the bathroom door.

'Hey, are you going to be long?' she asked.

I had had a very long trip. The night before the flight I hadn't slept at all, and I hadn't slept a wink on the plane either. Above all I was suffering from the effects of jet lag. And I still hadn't even had the chance to put my suitcase down.

The living room was covered with half-filled bottles of wine, glasses, plates, dirty cups with cigarette butts stuck in them, and dozens of overflowing ash-trays. It was about eleven in the morning.

After taking a shower, the Spanish girl, Victoria, went off to work. Lisa, somewhat more awake, came into the living room.

'You don't know how crappy I feel,' she said.

I asked her if she wanted a cup of tea. I went to the kitchen to fix it for her. I had to dislodge a cup from the pile of china that was stacked in the sink. The pots were stacked so high it was almost impossible to get at the water tap.

I took the tea to her in bed and asked her if she wanted any medicine. She said she did. I offered to look for a drugstore and to buy it.

'Bring me something that doesn't have codeine. They put codeine in everything in this country.'

I went down to the drugstore. It was my first morning in Madrid. Lisa's house was on a steep street in a working class neighborhood. Everything seemed dirty and poor and the day was very windy. The whirlpools of dust kept me from opening my eyes. Plastic bags and sheets of newspaper were blowing down the street. The medicine cost me a lot of money.

I gave the medicine to Lisa.

'Waa,' she said. 'Could you tidy up a bit. OK? Thanks. Agh. Shut the door, so I can sleep.'

I spent the next two hours cleaning and scrubbing the whole house. I washed the dishes, emptied the ashtrays, scoured pots with rice stuck to the bottom (they had had a paella party), and emptied the wine bottles, which I left neatly in a corner of the kitchen. When I had arrived I could barely stay on my feet, but house cleaning revived my energy. I took a shower and called the only person I knew in Madrid besides Lisa. He worked as a curator at the Caixa and asked me how I was doing.

'OK,' I answered. 'A bit tired, still suffering from the effects of jet lag.'

A little later, just before he hung up, he added, 'OK, listen then, why don't you call me when you get over that jet pack?'

Cohn vs Farber

Thomas Cohn ... arte contemporanea

29 June 1990

Fax to: BARBARA HUSSEIN ABU NIDAL EL ARAFAT C/O HEZBOLLAH-AGENCY
KHOMEINI-ISPHAHAN MARKET
IRAN

Dear Barbara,
As an Arab you don't get any discount at all. As a Jew we negoshit it.
Ve split and you get it for $ 16,500 bags. Who kerrs about money, ve dont vant
no money any wei.
Now, what are Jews with no money doing in French castles? Well, this is none
of my business.
Talking about business: whenever you have the money ready (say August)
please deposit it at:
THOMAS COHN
ISRAELI DISCOUNT BANK
XXXX
ACCOUNT N° XXXX-XXXX-XXX

Are you happy now, having robbed a Jew of $ 500 and of a Polish bed. Shame
on you. I hope this fax wakes you up and your bed conscience does not allow
you to sleep anymore.

Love,
Thomas

GALERIE BARBARA FARBER

30 June 1990   **33**

Fax to: Thomas Cohn
From: Barbara Farber

Dear Thomas,
I'm used to people with a weird sense of humor. Actually I thought it was quite
funny. (Or, I even thought it had a couple of good jokes.) I will take the bed at
16,5 although I still would prefer 16.
Would you arrange with Chris Dercon that it be delivered to the gallery in
Amsterdam. I don't know how organized he is but I can just see it getting back
to Brazil.
Please let me know if this has been arranged.
You can contact me at Chateau Shalom.

Regards,
Barbara

Allah be praised!!

The Hunter

Victoria has gone to work and Lisa is sleeping in her room under the effects of the codeine when someone knocks at the door.

'Who is it?' I ask.

'Your neighbor.'

I open and find a slight woman of about sixty who tells me, 'Look, what happened is that a package has arrived for Victoria Alvarez and since my surname is Alvarez they brought it to me, but I didn't accept it because my children don't let me open the door for anyone. I live alone, you see, so I sent it back.'

'So,' I say to her.

'That's all, just that, so if she is expecting a package, don't expect it anymore. Though perhaps the mailman will bring it back again in the afternoon.'

'That's a possibility,' I say, although I have no idea how the mail service functions in Spain. 'OK, thanks.'

'At your service,' she answers, and goes down the stairs.

At about 6:30 the mailman turns up with the package for Victoria Alvarez and, as there is no one else at home, I sign the register for it. He gives me the package which I put on the living room table. In the evening I go out and come back late. The girls are either sleeping or not at home. My sleep pattern is out of sync because of the 'jet pack,' and I decide to take some pills to help me sleep. But worried about the effect that so much medication is going to have on me, I don't manage to close my eyes the whole night.

The next day I go to El Prado. People are waiting in line for hours to see the Velázquez show and then leaving with two or three catalogues each. I decide to look at the permanent collection so as not to have to stand in line.

A guard says to me that he can't understand them.

'You see, we have all the important works by Velázquez hanging here all year long; with the exception of the mulata, the Venus of the mirror, and that little old lady frying eggs, the rest of the paintings that they've brought are run of the mill.'

On leaving the museum, I go into a book store and buy an appointment book for 1990. I jot on the first page: 'Call Raquel de la Concha. Call Jesús.'

When I reread the notation later about what I have to do that day and see those names, I know I can only be in Spain.

It's winter but in the street an African wind is blowing. It's already night and I decide to go back to Lisa's. I go down into the subway, which is packed with people, and, without realizing it, I block the exit of a woman who then stabs me with her elbow. I look at her with hate in my eyes, and she stomps on my foot and shouts, 'Spastic!'

People turn around and look at us. The woman walks away down the platform; the train's doors close, and I go on my way to the next station.

When I get back to Lisa's, Victoria opens the door for me. Lisa isn't there. Victoria points to the package that I had signed for the day before. It's back on the living room table. She tells me that neither she nor Lisa dare to open it because it is from Switzerland and a few days before Victoria had a fight with her boyfriend over the phone. Her boyfriend lives in Freiburg, and this is his response to the fight on the phone. She asks me to please open the package.

'He's a hunter, you see, and I am afraid of what it might be.'

Victoria tells me that she took the package to her room the night before and couldn't sleep thinking about the contents. The gift had come with a little note that said, 'This is for the conversation the other day.' She finally had to take the box out of her room in order to get to sleep.

I walk over to the table where the package is. It's about twelve inches by eight. Just about anything can be inside of it.

'Shall we throw it out?' Victoria asks.

I carefully unwrap the first layer of tape from the paper that covers the package. It's a cardboard box that's in pretty bad shape. I open it little by little. Inside there is foam rubber protecting something else, I can't guess what. It takes a while to get the foam rubber out because it has been squeezed in very tightly. I have to turn the box over on the table and I do it abruptly. Victoria lets out a cry and I, scared, jump back. There is still something else in the foam rubber; it is there on the table and I am afraid to touch it.

'It may be the teeth of a fish,' Victoria tells me.

I look at her surprised.

'I beat the fishing record in Nepal, you see, and he kept the teeth. Maybe now that we had a fight he wants to send them back to me.'

She goes over to the bookcase, looks for a gigantic fish scale and shows it to me.

'It was the first time I ever went fishing.'

I prod the foam rubber with a ballpoint pen. At first it seems soft enough, but I push harder and finally strike something solid.

'Shall we throw it out?' Victoria asks me once again. 'It could be anything.'

I don't pay any attention. I grab a corner of the foam rubber with my fingertips and pull, so that the contents spread out on the table. Inside there's a red handkerchief. But inside the handkerchief there is still something else.

'This is too much,' I say. 'Shall we throw it out?'

There's a pause. I approach the handkerchief, take it by one corner and open it on the table. I think maybe it's a finger, or the hoof of a wild boar. The man could have been desperate. But when the contents of the handkerchief finally fall onto the wooden table top the noise is a loud, sharp one, and Victoria and I stand there with our mouths open staring at a silver bracelet which, at either end, has a fish in relief, one looking at the other.

'Oh, this is beautiful,' Victoria says, and she tries it on.

*   *   *

Fifteen minutes later, while I'm in the kitchen washing the dishes, Victoria comes over and tells me, 'Listen, I want to tell you what happened to me. I was working for a gallery at ARCO, you know, and the owner of the gallery is a real handsome American, and from the very first day that we met there was this infatuation. I was turned on by him and he was turned on by me, and on that first day, I asked him, 'Have you been to Madrid before?' and he answered, 'Uh, yes, I'm married.' Instead of Madrid he had understood 'married'... Well, like during all these ten days we've exchanged winks, looks, all that sort of thing, and I was expecting the guy to do something once and for all, but nothing happened. Until tonight, the last day of ARCO, finally, we went out to dinner, just the two of us, tête à tête.

'We ordered dinner, then dessert, and finally liqueurs, but the guy didn't make his move. Time passed and I was getting tired, so I asked him, 'What are we going to do about it?' 'About what?' he answered me. 'Come on, you know very well what I am talking about'. 'I don't know what you mean, look...' So I got up from the table, grabbed a taxi and, furious, I came back here. Five minutes later the phone rang and it was the same guy wanting to tell me that I had received a letter from abroad at his hotel, and he took the opportunity to ask me if I was still angry. 'Of course,' I said. 'But why?' 'You know very well why.' 'No, I don't.' 'Mira, tío,' I said, 'because right now we should be making love in your hotel room.' And the guy went into shock and told me he didn't understand anything and all that sort of crap. He was speechless. 'I don't know what to say,' he told me when he got his voice back. 'This is so unusual.' So I hung up on him. That was five minutes before you got here. What do you think? Is the guy an idiot? Did I do the right thing? If a girl tells you that, how would you take it?'

I answer that it seems to me that she did what she had to do.

'It's that none of my friends would have lasted ten days with a guy that they like without doing something. I behaved like a saint. What do you think?'

'Well, everyone's different...'

'The guy's an asshole.'

'He's American.'

'And you, what would you think of a girl who acted like that with you?'

'Well, what's important is what he thinks, not what I think.'

'I'm asking you because I think you're a normal kind of guy...'

'Well, it wouldn't seem so strange to me... But I am not such a normal kind of guy...'

I start to open the sofa bed.

'Want me to help you set up the bed? What's your name?'

'Martin.'

'Good night, Martin.'

'Good night...'

I turned out the light and climbed in between the sheets. After a few minutes, Victoria opens the door to her room again, which is connected to the living room where I am and, without coming out of her room, asks me: 'Martin, do you think I should call the Swiss guy to thank him for the bracelet. It's beautiful... but, don't you think he's trying to buy me?'

*   *   *

I am still unable to overcome the insomnia. This time I increase the dosage of valerian: four tablets, and I decide I won't trust the natural way, adding two Valium. When I am just about to take a Calm Forté, the door opens and Lisa comes in. Victoria is already asleep, probably embracing her bracelet.

I tell her all of Victoria's story with her gallery owner and her Swiss boyfriend and she collapses on the floor in laughter. When she stops laughing, she sees the bottle I have in my hand and asks me, 'Hey, what have you there?'

'It's Calm Forté, a natural tranquilizer. Do you want one?'

'I've got to go out now. They invited me to Chicote for drinks. Ay, I don't know whether to take cocaine or that stuff you've got.'

'Calm Forté doesn't have codeine,' I tell her.

'What should I do?'

'Why don't you take the bottle in your bag and you can decide later?'

Lisa goes off to Chicote and takes my bottle. Later, when she comes back, I still haven't been able to sleep a wink.

'Hello.'

'Hello. I finally went to the Stella, and that guy Carpio chased me all over the place. He wouldn't leave me alone, I think he was trying to fondle me. I'm going to sue him. When I was leaving, he followed me down the stairs and asked me, shouting, what my sign was, and afterwards he told me he was certain that same day we were going to be friends.'

I listen to her and, now completely awake, ask her what she finally decided to take.

'Cocaine.'

The Cab Driver's Wife

Guillermo called me from Basel and he told me that they had published his catalogue at the Kunsthalle with all the pictures upside-down. The only thing that occurred to me to say was that the Swiss will stand on their heads in order to look at them right side up; that didn't seem to amuse him very much. He also told me that he had flown from Buenos Aires to Zurich where he was scheduled to take a train to Basel, but once he got there he decided to go by taxi. The distance from Zurich to Basel is about 60 miles and the taxi fare is a little over $ 300, but Guillermo managed to make a deal with the driver: He would go with him to his home, leave the taxi there and go in the cabbie's own car, thus getting himself driven to Basel for half the price.

The taxi driver's house was on the outskirts of Zurich, about 25 minutes from the airport. When they got there, a woman came out and greeted them, and the driver and the woman began to talk in a local dialect. Guillermo waited in the taxi. The driver came back and told him in English, 'We've got a problem. My brother-in-law, a good-for-nothing who lives with us and doesn't do anything at all, took my car; but he should be coming back any moment now.'

So the three of them went into the living room of the house. The woman served them all kirsch, and when she learned that Guillermo was a painter, and an Argentinean besides, she said, 'I am delighted, because that's two coincidences: I have spent a lot of time in Madrid and I also paint.'

The taxi driver got up from the table and went over to a pile of paintings that were stacked against the wall and turned the first around.

'What do you think?' he asked.

Guillermo told me that the man showed him, one by one, all the paintings his wife had painted with passionate brushstrokes of highly intense yellows and reds, completely different from the landscape of an industrial suburb of Zurich. The woman loved Spain, and her paintings were horrible.

'What do you think?' the driver kept asking.

An hour later the driver's brother-in-law returned, and since he was a good-for-nothing and didn't have anything to do, he went with Guillermo and the husband of his sister to the Kunsthalle in Basel.

Emotional Disturbances

Four days have gone by since I arrived in Madrid; I still haven't met anyone, I'm still flat broke, and Madrid still sucks. Lisa needs the house for herself and I look for somewhere else to stay. She goes for a long weekend to a hotel with a pool in the Canaries, invited to a seminar for 'New Collectors' where she'll be getting together with art critics, curators, artists and new collectors. As I am not sure where I am going to sleep tonight, I ask Victoria if I can leave my suitcase there. Victoria tells me: 'Put it under Lisa's bed; there's room there for your suitcase.'

I pack a bag with a few things, leave my suitcase where Victoria told me, and look for an inexpensive pension. I find one that isn't too bad on Barco Street and, as I am paranoiac about the phobia Spaniards have for Argentineans, when I register I try to speak like they do, emphasizing the differences between *c*'s and *s*'s a lot, but the only thing I achieve with my accent is that the owner asks me, 'Are you a Canary?' She's referring to the residents of the islands.

'Of course I am,' I answer. But she discovers the truth when I give her my passport.

'I was born in Buenos Aires because my parents were diplomats,' I say, justifying my previous statement. 'It was an accident.'

A week goes by and the African wind dies down. It gets colder every day and I left my leather jacket in the suitcase, so on Friday I go back to Lisa's house to look for it. I ask permission to go into her room, and when I take the suitcase from under her bed I hear a series of uncontrolled screams.

'What? That bag's yours? Take it away! Take it away! Take it away! Who gave you permission to put it there?'

At first I don't know exactly what she's talking about, but I soon realize Lisa wasn't there the day I left the suitcase. She gets angrier and angrier.

I explain that I asked her roommate, Victoria, for permission, but she continues yelling at me without being able to control herself. I ask for her forgiveness and apologize for the trouble I may have caused, and I also tell her that I have nowhere to take the suitcase to today and ask if I may please leave it at her house for one more day.

'No! No! No!' she yells.

Victoria, who was watching the scene in silence, says, 'I think there's room over the wardrobe, I'll have to look...'

'No! No! No!'

Finally, a bit calmer, Lisa says grudgingly, 'OK, you can leave it under my bed until Monday. Come and get it in the afternoon.'

Monday at 4:30 p.m. I ring the bell at Lisa's.

'What are you doing here at this time of day?' she growls at me when she opens the door.

'I've come to get my suitcase.'

'Agh, you don't want to let me get any work done; I told you to come in the afternoon.'

'It is the afternoon, Lisa, it's half past four.'

'That's not the afternoon, it's midday.'

'Oh,' I say, surprised. 'And when is it afternoon?'

'At 8:00.'

'I understand,' I reply, as if what she's saying to me is logical and natural. But she keeps on yelling at me.

'Almost without knowing you, I let you stay in my home and what do you do, you take advantage of my generosity. Someone gives you a hand and you take an arm; I'm not responsible for you Argentineans who are wandering around Europe with no place to stay.'

I try not to look her in the eye.

'Agh, I'm sick of living like a gypsy, I'm not that girl who locked herself up for two days in her room in Buenos Aires taking coke. And I'm not your secretary either; while you weren't here you've had five phone calls. Agh, Argentineans, if they're all like you, I can understand why you have a reputation in Europe.'

I try to explain to her. I ask her not to blame an entire country for my wrong-doings, not to use this specific situation to jump to such generalized conclusions. But she insists on her point of view. So to end the scene, I tell her that we belong to two different cultures and that we will perhaps never be able to reach a mutual understanding about everything, but that in spite of this, and above all, I don't want this episode to damage our friendship.

But Lisa insists.

'If we were in my country I'd sue you for emotional disturbances.'

This time nothing that I say seems to calm her down, not even the sociological arguments, nor the apologies, nor the promises. I am the sole target of her anger, which seems limitless.

'We can carry on like this for hours, Lisa,' I interrupt her, finally gathering energy, desperate to get back on to the street safe and sound with my suitcase. 'But I don't think that we're going to get anywhere. We have differing points of view. Why don't you want to get this over with, once and for all?'

'It's because you are going to go back to Buenos Aires now and you are going to tell all my friends that I treated you like a bitch,' she answers.

'I can assure you that you don't have to worry about that,' I tell her, placing my hand over my heart. 'I have absolutely no reason to ever talk about this matter to anyone. I swear this is just between you and me.'

Catholics from the Slums

Every so often Julia got a great idea. Once she decided to hire a woman who was to be in charge of *Julia Lublin Classics,* a new section of the gallery she had just created. Several candidates turned up for the position and finally Mrs. Graciela was chosen. Julia envisioned her as the ideal person for the job. She was to be in charge specifically of the administrative chores. She had the experience because she had run other galleries.

This woman stood out because of her age, her hardly refined features and, above all, for her devotion to a Miraculous Virgin. All these characteristics combined gave the gallery, with her presence, a very personal touch.

When you asked her about her Virgin, she sold her to you like she was a washing machine: 'Look,' she'd say, 'she is a very good Virgin; all you have to do to get her to work is light candles for her, pray to her, and when you ask her, she works miracles.'

As time passed, herbs and miraculous leaves appeared over some of the paintings, and small cards with religious prints of Argentinean saints could be found attached to many of the stretchers; it was supposed this procedure would increase the gallery's sales.

The devotion of this woman to her Virgin was so great that little by little Julia also began to believe in her almost magical powers, and if you called the gallery in the afternoon you could never get anyone to answer the phone because both of them had taken the car and gone to the Sanctuary, which was somewhere on the outskirts of Buenos Aires. Only they knew where.

The fame of the Virgin began to extend beyond the frontiers of the back room of the gallery and it wasn't long before everyone in the art world was talking about her. Many people laughed, but many wanted to see her, too. What no one could understand was how Julia, a woman so refined that you almost couldn't tell she was Jewish, could have fallen for this kind of Catholicism. In the beginning, Julia denied it all, but in the most difficult times, when the gallery was hopelessly going under, she began to call on the Virgin in public, and more directly. But the Virgin didn't help, not in that moment or in any other. And ever since that woman joined the gallery, not a single painting ever sold; and worse, the only picture that departed the gallery's premises in the 600 block of Marcelo T. de Alvear Street departed because it was stolen.

Marcia Schvartz and Her Headache

The other day Marcia called. She had a frightful headache and she said she had gone to her analyst and that the analyst had said her head ached because she had an idea that was about to hatch.

Marcia waited a day but the headache didn't go away and an idea didn't hatch either, so she decided to call her doctor. The doctor recommended that she take two Bayer aspirins.

The Little Worm

One day Christina Delancey and I made an appointment to meet at a cafe for opera freaks which was on 71st between Columbus and Central Park West. Christina has designed the logo by mail for my first film production company – now broke.

Christina is seated near the window and we don't have any problem recognizing each other, as usually happens when you make a date by phone and have never seen each other before. I ask for a *latte di mandorla* and as she couldn't make up her mind, I recommend she try the same. We talk about mutual friends and what we've read lately. Christina tells me she is reading *Foucault's Pendulum* and she doesn't seem very happy about it; there are several scenes that bother her because she's an animal rights advocate.

Christina, a long time ago, was the girl friend of Otto Grokenberger and was still his friend. It was Otto who had commissioned her to design the logotype for my production company.

Otto was the producer of the picture I had started to film in Buenos Aires, but one day he skipped town. The maid who cleaned the apartment we had rented for him called the office to ask where he had moved, because in the apartment everything was gone, even the china.

Afterwards they told me that the room was empty; nothing was left in the refrigerator and Otto had only left a book which I had lent him and a pair of old, very worn pants on the bare mattress. That's what they told me, because I refused to go up.

That same night we went to the home of Julio Raffo, the production company's lawyer. I expected the worst: My signature was at the bottom of every contract and obligation that we had signed in order to make the film. I missed ending up in jail by the skin of my teeth.

*   *   *

By her expression, I get the impression that Christina doesn't like the *latte di mandorla* and I have to keep telling myself it's not my fault; it's a drink that the majority of the people I know love. By way of an answer, she tells me she is horrified by the animal tortures Umberto Eco describes in full detail in his latest novel.

'Otto is a person with a lot of problems,' she tells me, finally getting down to the nitty-gritty. I was anxious to hear these reports. 'He just did what he did to you to a director in Texas. They organized the production and then one fine day he just vanished without letting anyone know.'

'Ah.'

'After your picture, he hid out in New York and wouldn't go out on the street. Everyone wanted to know what had happened in Argentina. He said that he had had to escape because you and the director of photography had kidnapped him and he had been held incommunicado for a week.'

'Ah,' I say.

'Since they were asking him too many questions in New York, he had to go off to Munich with his wife. They had gotten married four or five months before.'

'Yes, I remember someone mailed me an invitation.'

'Otto's wife returned to New York before he did, and when Otto joined her again, she told him she was leaving him. She had joined a sect that believed that Jesus Christ was Japanese and flew to Japan on a flying saucer.'

'Ah,' I say, and I see that Christina gets that disgusted look again. 'It's only milk with almond extract.' I try to calm her.

'What?'

'Your drink.'

When we go out to the street, it's pouring. We are both going the same direction and we walk several blocks together.

'A lot of people in the business don't believe a word of what he said when he came back from Argentina,' Christina tells me from under her umbrella, and then she bends down at the edge of the sidewalk to pick something up.

'Otto is a person with a lot of problems,' she repeats.

When Christina stands up again, I see she has a worm in her hand. She takes it over to the entrance of a building and leaves it in a flower bed that is protected from the storm; and so she saves the worm from a certain death by rain.

Armani vs Kuitca

In the middle of 1990, at the opening of a painting exhibit in Buenos Aires, a stranger came up to Guillermo and said, *Nadie olvida nada.*

Guillermo looked at him a bit disconcerted and finally answered him, making gestures of agreement and compliance, 'Ah, that's right, for sure.'

'I have a painting of yours,' said the man, who was neither short nor tall and in no way unusual. The only detail that distinguished him was an overcoat hanging from his shoulders in such a way that you could read the enormous label that said 'Giorgio Armani' very clearly, and his shirt also had 'Armani' written on it in large letters.

'That's fine, all right, there are people who I don't know that have bought pictures of mine,' Guillermo continued to agree.

'I stole a painting of yours.'

This time Guillermo didn't answer him, because he didn't know if the man was serious or not.

'I have the little yellow bed and I stole it from that fanatic fundamentalist who worked at Julia's, and I stole it from her because she's such an asshole.'

Guillermo asked Sonia Becce, his secretary, for a pen as she happened by, and he wrote down the stranger's address and telephone number.

'Tomorrow I'll come and get it.'

'I was thinking of returning it to Annina,' the man said. 'I used to work in art galleries. I didn't want to return the picture to those two...'

'Listen to me, Annina sued a guy for putting up a poster with her name on it in Costa Rica. Do you need that?'

'I am a very good friend of one of the curators at the Whitney. He was going to give the painting to Annina, but I found out from a lot of people who know you that you're an OK guy.'

*　　*　　*

The next day Guillermo asked Sonia to call the thief in order to get the picture back. It was never clear how the picture had actually disappeared from the gallery. They supposed it was during a party at which there were a multitude of people, in the time of the Virgin. Guillermo suspected the disc jockey, and a few days after the robbery was discovered, he made a trip to New York that coincided with the theft of a picture by Stephen Müller at Annina's gallery.

Guillermo found out that Annina had hired a detective to investigate the case and it seemed to him like a good idea to check up on the disc jockey and his girl friend in the same way. But on returning to Buenos Aires Julia told him, without having any kind of evidence at all, that she suspected Sonia.

When Sonia called the real culprit of the robbery, the man hung up immediately, scared that it might be a legal intimation, and immediately called Guillermo, very frightened.

'Please, all I want to do is give you back the painting; I'll bring it to your studio.'

When he got there, the man rang the bell, handed Guillermo a package, and without even going in, turned right around and left.

The picture was wrapped in old newspapers. Guillermo unwrapped it and saw that it was stained with spaghetti sauce. He went out into the hallway; the stranger was still there, because the door to the building was locked.

'Hey, you ate on top of this painting.'

'Screw you,' answered the man dressed in Armani. 'And when you want to exhibit at Mary Boone's, call me.'

They steal your painting, they give it back all fucked up, you complain and they say 'screw you', Guillermo thought; and for the first time since the whole affair had started, something amused him.

La Pelu

La Pelu had been the Argentinean consulese in Rio and now she had turned art dealer. That was how Sonia, Eduardo Alvarez and I ended up going out to dinner with her one night.

We were invited by the director of the Brazilian-Argentinean Cultural Institute, a charming lady whose name was May Lorenzo Alcalá. First we went to her home where we were given something to drink, and May's maid, a very old woman named Dona Seguinha, took pictures of us in all sorts of twisted poses; she threw herself on the floor and climbed on the furniture like she was a fashion photographer.

From there we all went to eat at a very good restaurant with a view over the bay and, after dinner, May gave me three books that she had written.

Late at night, when we got back to the hotel, Sonia, Eduardo and I went to my room to read. First each of us read our favorite story out loud, I don't know what we had drunk or done, but we were very amused; one of the books was ritually stripped of its pages and we let the pages float out over Ipanema Beach; and, as it was unbearably hot, at one point we put the other two books in the freezer of the Frigobar.

The next day Susy, Thomas' wife, took us to see the beaches of Rio. We started the tour in Ipanema and didn't get out of the car once; we sat in silence the whole trip and she, with her forehead glued to the car window, described what we saw in a sort of nostalgic litany.

'Polluted, not polluted, polluted, not polluted...'

That night the show opened. Sonia, Eduardo and I went to the hotel to change, and then we took a taxi.

When we got to the gallery and the driver asked for fifteen times more than what the fare should have been, we offered to pay him what the meter said or nothing at all. Sonia and I got out and the driver took off, kidnapping Eduardo who, as he was in the middle, didn't have time to get out of the car. Sonia and I ran like crazy, shouting in desperation in our fractured Portuguese, 'Nosso amigo! They've kidnapped nosso amigo!'

The car stopped two hundred yards away and the driver freed Eduardo, who had already given him all the money he had, besides his leather jacket.

That was one of the reasons why Eduardo Alvarez returned ahead of schedule to Buenos Aires. A few days later, when Sonia and I flew over Southern

Brazil, I struck my head with the palm of my hand, looked at Sonia and yelled, 'The books!'

I thought of that moment of total disconnection when we had frozen those books; the act seemed to be as divorced from reality as the gesture by that woman in New York who, when she interviewed me for *Bomb* magazine, brought me, as a present, a bottle of shampoo. For an instant my head went back to Rio: A tourist decides to put an ice cube in his Guarana and he finds May Lorenzo Alcalá's stories frozen in the Frigobar.

David and Ana Jauregui's Maid

I knew that David Leavitt was in Spain thanks to one of those programs of the Generalitat de Catalunya, but I didn't know how to get in touch with him. That day I went to a gallery that specialized in work by young artists. They had called me about a picture I had by a Spanish painter, which might be of interest to one of their clients.

There is a very young American working as secretary in the gallery and at one point I comment out loud, 'I'm really upset because David Leavitt is giving a lecture today at the American Institute and I can't go to it.'

The American turns around and looks at me bewildered, as if he were asking himself what the hell it matters to this lady, who is selling such expensive pictures, that David Leavitt is giving a lecture.

When I am about to leave the gallery, the secretary comes over and asks me, 'Do you like David Leavitt?'

'A lot,' I answer. 'I love him. I've read all his books. And besides, at home, I have a painting by an Argentinean painter titled *The Lost Language of Cranes*.

'I am going to the lecture. Do you want me to give him a message?'

'Get him to come to my home. Leavitt can't leave Madrid without seeing that painting.'

'Give me your phone number.'

That night, when I get home, I find a message on the answering machine from the American secretary. 'David is very enthusiastic, excited, and anxious to see the picture.'

I call back and we agree to get together the next evening at 8:00.

*   *   *

Hector wanted me to give Leavitt some important material about AIDS and invite him to the 4th International Congress on AIDS victims which was to be held in Madrid. So I tell Hector and Ricardo to come too and we begin getting ready for that night. By 1:00 midday we knew exactly what we were going to do: Eduardo had reserved a table at the Excelsior; we already had the cars in which we could get around; we had decided first to have a coffee, then drinks, and I had found out the most 'in' discotheques. At 1:25 the phone rings. It's John, the secretary.

'I'm sorry, Ana, but I have bad news. David is desperate, because Almodóvar just invited him for a showing at 8:00. He asked if he can come by at 3:00?'

It was completely impossible for me to be at home at 3:00 in the afternoon and I knew the others were busy too. And Leavitt was leaving early the next morning.

Isabel, my maid, who was ironing in the kitchen, sees me so upset that she comes over and asks, 'Señora Ana, is something wrong?'

'John, I'll call you in five minutes,' I tell the secretary. 'Look, Isabel, if you can stay a bit longer, I'll pay you.'

'What do I have to do?'

'Show some pictures.'

'Ay, that's great.'

I call John and confirm the meeting between David Leavitt and my maid at 3:00 in the afternoon and then I dedicate myself to educating Isabel.

'A man who's a writer is coming; he wrote these books... And that picture...'

'Ah, yes, Guillermo's picture.'

'Is about this book.'

'And what's this about cranes?'

'I'll explain that to you right away.'

'And that apartment?'

'Guillermo imagined that what happens in the book happens in that apartment.'

'So, what do I have to do?'

'You show the picture and give him these three books that he wrote so that, if he wants to, he can dedicate them to me. This is material about AIDS that he has to take with him, and if he wants to see more of Guillermo's pictures, take him to the back where there's another one,' and I leave, really freaked out by it all.

About 4:00 in the afternoon, I call Isabel.

'They just left.'

'How'd it go?'

'Marvelously. There were two of them. I gave them the stuff on AIDS and they wrote a beautiful dedication and they also left their addresses. They went all over the house, even the bedroom. And how they gossiped!'

'And the picture?'

'They loved it, especially the one with glasses.'

That night, as planned, we all got together at my home.

'And Leavitt?'

'He's not coming.'

'And the picture?'

'He's already seen it.'

'How?'

'I'll explain it all to you now.'

Since we'd made the reservation, the four of us went to dine at the Excelsior, and during the meal I told Hector, Ricardo and Eduardo all that had happened that afternoon between Isabel and David Leavitt.

Western Vegetarian

I was looking at a Chilean woman. She had a baby carriage with twins and also led another little boy, about two, on a leash. The child on the leash banged his fist against the large windows of dark glass that overlooked the runways, incessantly and joyfully shouting 'motherfucker, motherfucker.' His mother didn't say anything to him. A uniformed man came up to them and the child yelled motherfucker at him too.

At the gate I noticed a couple of very old Calabrian peasants. They both used canes and the woman shouted as if the whole world was deaf as well.

Once on the plane, I found I was sitting in the row in front of the Calabrians and across the aisle from the Chilean woman with the twins and the child on the leash. Alongside of them was a couple with two more babies that never stopped crying. When the child on the leash saw the stewardess, he said to her, 'hi, motherfucker' and the Dutch stewardess just smiled.

In Montevideo the only people that boarded were 60-year-old women who were traveling with their mothers. They must have been part of some tour. One of them said 'Excuse me' in English, and sat down beside me. Now I was surrounded by Chileans, Uruguayans and Calabrians. It was too soon for me to feel like such a foreigner.

One of the Uruguayan women came down the aisle until she reached my seat and looking back at her friends seated in the rows in the back of the plane, shouted to them, 'Here are the bathrooms.'

At that moment the stewardess appeared and the woman asked her in English, 'Which is the channel for classical music?'

'Number seven,' the stewardess replied.

'It's number seven!' the woman shouted in Spanish toward the rear of the plane. She must have been the tour guide.

I was thrown off when my meal arrived before any of the others. The stewardess brought me the tray by hand, not on one of the carts. All of the Chileans, Calabrians, and Uruguayans who surrounded me turned and fixed their eyes on me. At first they managed to intimidate me, but I decided to start eating anyway.

My meal consisted of rice, potatoes, pasta and some boiled vegetables, all without any condiments. The tray didn't even include those little packets of salt and pepper. I wasn't very hungry and the flavor of the food was horrible, but in spite of that, I managed to eat everything and I started to stack the plastic dishes so the stewardess wouldn't scowl at me. Under the platter that had held the main course, I found a label which said:

KLM Special Meal
Rejtman
Western Vegetarian
KL794 / 26 Sept.
Eze-Ams

It must have been a joke some friend played on me.

A little later, when the stewardesses came by offering tea or coffee, the Uruguayan woman asked for both.

It seems that Thomas Cohn had come on the same flight from Buenos Aires, because I found him in the hallway of the airport in Rio, walking toward the area reserved for in-transit passengers. I didn't recognize him right away, and then discovered that it actually was him; he had dyed his hair red. According to Sonia, this is the second time that he has dyed it.

Thomas walked on my left and spoke to me, but the plane's descent had clogged my ears, leaving me completely deaf on that side. At first I tried to read his lips, but I had to confess what had happened to me.

'Squeeze your nose and blow,' Thomas instructed me with gestures as we got to the point where the hallway split and we went our separate ways.

I squeezed my nose and blew, but I still felt the pressure in my ears and I couldn't hear anything. I was traveling with the sound tapes of the picture I had shot in Buenos Aires and on reaching the X ray control station, I wouldn't let the authorities pass the tapes through the machine.

'What's that?' I was asked in Portuguese.

I didn't know how to answer them until I had an inspiration and, partly because of my enthusiasm for having remembered the word in Portuguese and partly because of my deafness, I shouted hysterically in their tongue, 'Fitas! Fitas!!'

And they let me through.

I spent the forty minutes between flights in Galeao glued to my seat, hugging my tapes, squeezing my nose and blowing. Then, once on the plane again, and in spite of Insomnium, a tranquilizer which had just been banned in Argentina that I'd bought with a faked prescription Guillermo had given me, I didn't manage to sleep a wink the entire flight.

I traveled to Holland at the end of September with the illusion that, at a time of year when the climatic differences were less perceptible, there were fewer contrasts in the world. The beginning of spring in the Southern Hemisphere mingles with the end of winter and coincides with the beginning of autumn in the North, a time still contaminated by the last days of summer.

Racism, Homophobia and Misogyny

One freezing dawn in the middle of February, I took a plane from the airport in New York and landed a few hours later in a southern American city where the climate was much warmer. The director of the university's art department was coming to get me because I had been invited to give a seminar for the art students. I didn't know him, and he didn't know me either, so, as can be expected, we didn't find each other, because there was no one there holding a piece of cardboard with my name handwritten on it. I was forced to seek the help of some nuns, who first announced my name on the loudspeaker system. When no one appeared to claim me, they called the university to send for someone.

Twenty minutes later a man arrived who picked up my bags, and said something like, 'Ollw i ta ta ca,' and headed for the door on the run. The accent in the South is very distinctive, and the only English I understand is what they talk in New York, so to everything the man said to me during the trip to the hotel, I answered alternating two phrases: 'I'm sorry, I don't understand' and 'Certainly.' When I had to say goodbye at the Georgia Inn, he took my arm firmly and told me, 'Wull a yum ol tem a bians.'

'I'm sorry, I don't understand.' It was my turn to reply, and I smiled, because now the little game was beginning to amuse me.

The hotel seemed straight out of *Gone with the Wind*. I was impressed by how different the South was. There were no blacks, not even as cashiers; they only carried bags or swept the floor. They seemed to have no contact with either money or people. On registering I was on the verge of asking the woman who owned the hotel if the man who brought me was the director of the art department, but I decided to keep my mouth shut.

On my first night the university had organized a dinner to which ex-President Alfonsín had been invited as well, but at the last moment he called to say that his wife María Lorenza had the flu. So we dined without Alfonsín on the first floor of a local restaurant, and his place was occupied by a lady who talked nonstop and who, from what I could understand, was president of an organization that involved the students at the university. The man who had picked me up at the airport was seated at the same table.

The next day I began visiting artists' studios. I had two fantasies about the comments I was going to have to make to the students. One was: 'Oh, Geoffrey, what a beautiful jar you've painted today!,' 'Oh, Lora, what lovely sunflowers you've done this afternoon!'

And another: 'Oh, Geoffrey, what fine coordinates you've found in that mountain!,' 'Oh, Lora, what a beautiful hole in the wall you've perforated this week!'

I realized right away that I was going to have to put my second fantasy into practice with these artists.

They were mostly women, and what surprised me was how similar their work was to that of other American female artists who used texts in their works. I never pay much attention to the texts, generally I believe that a text is an image and I either like it or not in relation to how it holds up within the context of the painting. But in this case they all wrote so much that I had the impression there was some message that I was missing. The few males in the class were generally sculptors. One of them, for example, had destroyed the wall of his studio and that was his work. Another was so obsessed by the death of an uncle who perished in a plane crash that he had gone to Germany and found fragments of the wrecked aircraft. These men were totally marginal and appeared to be fed up with the women and their texts.

At about 4:00 in the afternoon I called for a tea break and sat by myself in the university's cafeteria to think. I decided to dedicate more attention to the meaning of the words in the works of these women. The man who had taken me from the airport to the Georgia Inn came into the cafeteria, walked over and, without asking, sat down at my table.

'D ya si?' he said.

'Certainly,' I answered, upset because he was interrupting my thoughts.

'Wull a yum ol tem a bians,' is what I understood.

'I'm sorry, I don't understand,' I said and got up with my tray, all set to change tables.

'Wull a yum ol tem a bians,' he repeated to me, wildly, trying to make me stay, but I still couldn't understand a single word he was saying, not this creep nor any of these Southern girls who wrote enigmatic phrases on their paintings.

I finished my tea at another table and went back to finish my rounds of the studios and, linking the phrase that the man had told me in the cafeteria, which had kept going around in my head, with the meaning of what these women had written, I realized that the texts were explicit declarations of lesbianism.

I was sorry not to have known this from the beginning, because from that moment on I enjoyed the work much more. Reading between the lines, I was able to discover which women formed couples; the pictures of one artist mentioned when she and another student had been together; there were works done jointly; the name of one woman was crossed out of the works of the other. Now that I knew what was going on, I was able to visit the remaining studios better prepared to register additional information about the movement. When I came upon a neo-figurative artist I was happy that, in spite of it all, things were not quite as simple as they seemed. Instead of telling her story in words she was telling it in images, and if she painted two figures making love, it was not easy to tell if the brushstroke was the face of a man or a woman.

The next day I had to give a lecture to all the students. It was without an interpreter and, in a way, I lost the thread of the things I was going to say. I wanted to make jokes, but it was tough for me in English and no one understood them; fortunately the atmosphere was pleasant.

That afternoon the man who had originally picked me up took me back to the airport. I still had no idea whether he was a lowly clerk or the director of the art department. When we got to the parking lot, he took a little piece of paper out of his pocket and read the Spanish translation of the phrase he had tried to say to me so many times.

'Certainly,' I replied, wanting to choke him to death, and for the first time I could see the look of concern disappear from his eyes. I grabbed my two bags and, without saying goodbye, walked toward the airport terminal building.

So schlafen unsere Sünden ein

I should have suspected something. The week before Roberta Smith had visited the show and, the same afternoon, ran into Finita on the street.

'Too many maps and not enough house plans,' she complained.

'When he makes maps, they want house plans and when he makes house plans, they want maps,' Finita answered, and went on her way.

Probably intrigued by Finita's statement, Roberta decided to go back and see the show again. I just happened to be in the gallery at the time and I saw her come in. Terrified, I hid behind a wall that she would inevitably have to pass in order to see a painting that was hanging on the other side.

That's how we knew that on Friday a review would be published in *The New York Times* and, Thursday night, consumed with anxiety, the four of us went to a newsstand on Sixth Avenue that sold newspapers earlier than anywhere else. I went with Eduardo Alvarez, Finita and a psychoanalyst friend of Finita's in a very small car. I got out to buy the paper and as soon as I got back in the car I began to read out loud. One skims something that's so crucial very quickly at first, looking for a phrase that stands out, and I did that at the same time that I was reading out loud for the others. All of a sudden I saw the word 'awful' coming up but I didn't stop, and the moment that I pronounced it there was an ominous silence in the car. Roberta Smith had written that there were some works that were 'really awful' hanging in the gallery. Someone immediately took the paper out of my hands and everyone began to snatch at it at once.

'In New York 'awful' is often used to say 'great,'' Finita said to calm me.

'You must have read it wrong,' Eduardo said.

'We could publish a letter to the editor in the next issue of *Lacanian Ink*,' the psychoanalyst suggested.

'The second issue just came out; the next number won't be on sale for four months,' Finita countered. She was editor of the magazine.

I couldn't stand it any more, I was getting asphyxiated so I asked them to let me out of the car. I felt that it was the end; the world was falling apart around me. I thought of my mom in her English class searching the dictionary for the word 'awful'; she, my Aunt Dorita and the teacher spend all the time chatting in Spanish, except when they have a magazine with an article about me, then they take advantage of the class in order to translate it.

The next day I got out of bed with my mind made up and reserved a flight back to Buenos Aires. My career in New York had ended. Before going back, fulfilling a final wish, I wanted to go and see Pat Hearn and buy a very dramatic work by Gretchen Faust that I had seen in her gallery; they were prayers to the Lord.

Pat Hearn turned out to be an angelical woman, just like Carole Bouquet. I was very nervous but she inspired so much confidence in me that I told her what was happening. It seemed like she was from another planet. She told me to keep cool, she advised me not to take it too seriously because it wasn't really important, she sold me her prayers and I went away feeling cheered up.

The work I had seen in the gallery was composed of two series of small bronze plaques installed in a corner. The verses of the prayers were in German and were engraved on each plaque. Since the bronze was highly polished, the plaques that were hanging on one wall were reflected in those hanging on the other and vice versa; the result was an image in the form of a cross. But, once back in Buenos Aires, when I opened the box Pat Hearn had given to me, I found only one of the series. I was crestfallen and felt I had deceived myself. How could I have interpreted the artist so badly?

Time passed. News from New York was encouraging. A lot of people had gone to see the show, maybe because the word 'awful' had piqued their curiosity, and all the important pictures had sold. One day a letter came from Pat Hearn. She said she realized that she had given me only part of what I had bought, and that she was going to send the rest by mail.

But when the second part of Gretchen Faust's work arrived in Buenos Aires, it went straight into the customs' warehouse; so Sonia had to go and get it out.

'What is this?' the surprised agent asked on opening the box.

For tax reasons Sonia couldn't explain that it was a work of art; even though in reality it was only half a work of art; it was nothing. Besides, as all the plaques looked alike, Sonia thought the woman might think that they had been bought wholesale.

'I'm a member of a religious organization and these are the prayers we give to each member of the sect,' she explained.

In order to prove it, the woman read one of the German verses out loud; after that she asked Sonia to advise the organization in the States that the next time they declare the shipment as 'religious plaques,' and she let Sonia take the prayers.

The two boxes sat forgotten and unopened in a corner of my room for two years, waiting for my new house to be finished. Then, not long ago, just back from a trip, I found the prayers in the trash can in the kitchen; I rescued them just a few minutes before they were to be taken to the street to be picked up by the garbage truck. Every time I travel, at home they decide to tidy up my room for me.

Bullewijk

In November I was in Amsterdam editing my film. This coincided with Guillermo's show at Barbara Farber's. One day Guillermo took a cab to visit me in the place where I was working and he pretended to be me.

'To Bullewijk.'

'That's a long way from here.'

'Yes, I know that.'

'Are you going there to work?'

'Yes.'

'What do you do?'

'I'm editing a movie. I'm a film director.'

'What's your picture called?'

'It doesn't have a title yet.'

'Do you like the work?'

'It gets tiring at times. It's very stressful.'

Guillermo and the driver remained silent for awhile; then, the taxi driver started talking about painting.

'I don't like Van Gogh.'

'I do,' Guillermo responded.

'I like Karel Appel.'

'Do you like Vermeer?'

'I like some pictures but not all of them, the same with Rembrandt. I liked *Godfather* III, *Sophie's Choice* and *The Sting*. And Robert Redford and Paul Newman, and *The Deer Hunter*. Al Pacino and Robert de Niro are the best. And the one who shoots himself at the end...'

'Christopher Walken.'

'I once took him for a tour of Amsterdam in this very car. I've had three letters from him already.'

'Where did he send them from?'

The driver didn't answer and instead asked, 'What's your film about?'

'About what goes on in the street, petty crime, all that... two kids in the city in today's world.'

'Cities everywhere have something in common.'

Guillermo and the driver were getting to Bullewijk, an ultra-modern suburb of intelligent buildings on the outskirts of Amsterdam.

Annina's Business with Sonia

Well, she never knows what to order. In Kassel we had to meet to talk about several different things. We went together to have ice cream and it was a disaster.

In Rotterdam we also had to talk; she wanted to see the photos of the artists that I represent. We were at the Witte de With and we crossed over to a Vietnamese place where there wasn't anything to drink, not even soft drinks, or tea or coffee. I didn't order anything, she didn't know what to order. She finally bought a plastic bag with a fried banana in it. It was floating in grease, and she ate it all. I didn't eat anything and on top of it all, I had to pay for the banana.

This time in Germany she wanted to look at the portfolios of my artists again. We made a date to meet the next day in a cafe. Annina arrived with a young collector who wholesaled clothing. He wanted to sell me garments and I wanted to sell him paintings. And Annina once again didn't know what to order. So she asked for an ice cream in German, and the waiter brings her a cup full of liquid with a floating ball of who knows what that seemed to be frozen. She gives it a try and makes an expression indicating supreme disgust. There was a guy at the next table and she asked him if he spoke English. He said he spoke French.

'What do you think? You see the crap they brought me?'

Then she took the ball of ice cream and put it on the saucer, and poured the liquid into a cup.

And we all participated in the show: the man at the other table looked at the photos of my artists, I skimmed the catalogue of clothing, the collector ate Annina's ball of ice cream, and Annina drank the liquid in the cup.

Kuitca vs Lublin

I had begun to have problems with Julia because when I went to ask her for the money she owed me, she used to cry and ask me to come back later. This went on for two years, more or less, until at one point Julia refused to talk and began to not answer my calls. It coincided with the time that the gallery was in bankruptcy, the period of the Catholics from the Slums.

We knew that my paintings had ended up in a storeroom. I was very worried about these pictures, especially one of them, *La busca de la felicidad,* because I had learned that it was no longer in Julia's possession; it had gone to the home of a collector. In those days I used to jog in Palermo Chico and I had a constant obsession: If I looked through all the windows at the interiors of these homes, I was going to see *La busca de la felicidad* through one of the windows.

We only knew the telephone number of the place where Julia had hidden my pictures, and I was determined to get the address at any price. My cousin Miriam has a boyfriend whose brother is a policeman and we tried to get the address through him, by cross-checking the phone number; but the attempt failed. I was getting more worried every day.

It was then that it occurred to me to send my father as an emissary, but Julia also refused to take his phone calls. So my dad, tired of getting the run-around, went and rang her doorbell, and Julia had no choice but to talk to him. At the end of their conversation, she told my father to have me call her.

The following week Julia and I got together, and she took me straight to the storeroom where she kept my paintings. 'Here are your paintings,' she said. 'You needn't be so worried.' I breathed deeply and felt relieved, because none were missing; even *La busca de la felicidad* was there.

It was at that moment that Julia said to me: 'I am going to sign a receipt saying I have all these pictures on consignment from you,' and I, in a gesture of trust and friendship, answered her, 'No, Julia, don't worry. We're just fine like this.' This is an image that still tortures me, even today. If I had that paper signed by Julia, all that happened afterwards could have been avoided.

*   *   *

One afternoon, at Julia's request, I went to her office on Maipú Street, where I inspected the works of Guillermo's that were in the storeroom and priced each of the pictures. It seemed like the relationship between the two of them had finally got back on track.

But not long after, I called her because Guillermo wanted to get his works back and Julia answered me with one of her most famous phrases, 'Tell Guillermo to stop screwing around.'

That phrase ended any chance of dialogue and we decided to look for a lawyer. Guillermo wanted to take drastic measures; he was very hurt by that famous phrase.

We went to Helft for advice and I met with him and with Daniel Martinez, who at that moment was advising Ruth Benzacar. Everything was kept very secret because if Julia found out, she would hide the paintings somewhere else. We had to act swiftly and decisively.

Daniel Martinez recommended that we see Dr. Alconada Aramburú, who had been Minister of Education and Justice under Alfonsín. We felt he was a sufficiently overwhelming figure and would prove we were really serious.

I called for an appointment and it was scheduled for two weeks later. When the day finally arrived, no one expected us. The secretary didn't know anything about our appointment, we weren't in the appointment book, but even so, she asked us to go into a waiting room and told us that the doctor was due to arrive shortly.

We immediately realized we were out of place in this office. The waiting room looked like a cabinet minister's office; the seats were easy chairs upholstered in cherry-colored leather and the walls were covered with diplomas and little pictures of Argentinean battle scenes. According to Guillermo, the place was super goy.

Time passed and Alconada Aramburú didn't appear. We were indignant for the first fifteen minutes, but then we immediately began to feel relieved. After forty-five minutes had passed we went and asked the secretary if we could use the telephone, and right on the spot we called some young lawyers that had been recommended to Guillermo. Without hesitating, we made an appointment with Rosenkrantz and walked over to his office. It was the day we had set aside to visit lawyers and, if the first one we'd chosen wasn't there, we'd go see another.

Guillermo painted a verbal portrait of Julia for Rosenkrantz who said, given the characteristics of her personality, it would be necessary to take drastic measures, because she might react out of rage. We decided then and there to take a precautionary measure: seize the paintings.

*   *   *

In May I introduced Guillermo to a lawyer. Not long after, early one morning, he calls me on the phone.

'We've been authorized to raid Julia's office to get the paintings back.'

'I'll meet you there with my notebook,' I said and hung up.

On the corner of the courthouse, I find Guillermo and the lawyers (Rosenkrantz, Zbar & Bouzat). The place is full of reporters and TV cameras because at any moment the President's sister-in-law, accused of trafficking narco-dollars, is about to appear. We are in the eye of the storm and we flee in a taxi to Julia Lublin's office.

An Officer of Justice and the Judicial Locksmith are waiting for us in the hallway in front of the office.

'We can begin to place the embargo on Mr. Lublin in relation to the pictures of the painter Guillermo Kuitca,' the Officer of Justice pronounces. 'If Mr. Lublin were to be present in his offcie at the moment of the seizure, he would automatically become the legal trustee for the embargoed pictures,' he warns us, pushing the buzzer by the door.

No one answers.

The Locksmith begins to prepare his drill to violate the lock, but there is no plug in the hallway. We decide to ring the neighbor's bell. He allows us to plug the drill in there.

While drilling the lock, the Locksmith tells us that he has often been thrown out in similar situations. Realizing that something unusual is happening when he hears the drill, the superintendent comes over to find out what is going on. We are all afraid that he'll call Julia to tell her about the raid and that Julia will rush over in a taxi. Something can still go wrong. We have to get the job over with very quickly.

The lawyers, the Officer of Justice, the neighbor, Guillermo, Guillermo's helper who just turned up, and I all watch the Locksmith drill. To reduce the tension a bit we separate in small groups to chat. I am with Carlos Rosenkrantz and the Officer of Justice. Carlos introduces me as a movie director and the Officer of Justice comments that the son of his partner is also a movie director; when he tells me the name, the person turns out to be a friend of mine and, besides, both Guillermo and I know the partner of the Officer of Justice very well. A spontaneous and friendly camaraderie springs up between all of us.

The Locksmith listens to us talk about the movies and, not to be excluded from the conversations, drill in hand, says to me that he could tell us more stories than you could fit in a TV series. Once the lock is forced and the door is open, we are ready to start the raid on the storeroom. But the moment we start going in, the phone starts ringing. We all freeze in our footsteps. No one can be calling this place at this time. It's an office no one ever uses. For as long as we listen to the rings, there is absolute silence; all eyes are glued to the telephone. Our breathing relaxes when it stops ringing.

According to the law, we are authorized to embargo the paintings whose title is written somewhere on the work. This title has to coincide exactly with the one that appears on the list originally presented to the judge. But *Un taller para el joven Kuitca* appears as *Un taller para Kuitca* and *Vaga idea de una pasión* as *Idea de una pasión*. And there are other cases, plus the paintings that don't even have a title written on their stretchers.

Thanks to the harmonious atmosphere in which we are working, the Officer of Justice lets Guillermo send his helper to buy a marking pen, with which he then corrects the mismatching titles and adds the nonexistent ones. One by one the sixteen pictures whose fate had so worried Guillermo appear and their titles get corrected as needed. When the inventory is finished, everyone helps carry them out and unload them in the office of the lawyer, who the judge had named the legal trustee. The paintings are stored in a bathroom that isn't being used. Rosenkrantz cuts off the water, seals the door hermetically and double locks it. To celebrate the outcome we all go to eat at an Arab vegetarian restaurant.

After lunch Rosenkrantz calls Julia on the phone to inform her of the sequestration and lets her know that the lock on her office has been changed and that the new keys are being held in custody at the courthouse. With great presence of mind she thanks him for the call and hangs up. Three minutes later Rosenkrantz's phone rings. It's a Dr. Herrera, who says that he doesn't know Mrs. Lublin very well, she's a client who was referred to him by a mutual friend, but that the woman is in a state of nervous shock, and he can't even get her to talk. The only information Dr. Herrera could get out of Julia was the name of Rosenkrantz and now he wants to know from Rosenkrantz exactly what happened.

One day, at 3:00 in the afternoon, the buzzer at the law office rings. When the secretary asks, 'Who is it' a voice answers. 'Giménez.' Teresita opens the door and, along with the so-called Giménez, five other thugs push their way into the office, tie up Rosenkrantz, Zbar & Bouzat, hands and feet, along with a telephone repairman who happened to be there, and take them one by one to the bathroom where they stack them one on top of the other. A human pile. They also tie up Teresita and gag her, but they leave her seated in the bathtub. They take the computers, faxes, telephones and decorative objects. It all happens very quickly and at first Rosenkrantz thinks the thieves were hired to steal the paintings. Six thugs to rob four computers and a fax. When they find the safe they ask for the key and empty it. The safe is a yard from the door to the small storeroom. But the thugs go by that door with total indifference; not one of them bothers to check on what there may be inside.

*   *   *

I think that Julia's lawyer made a mistake in legal tactics. I spoke with Dr. Herrera on the phone a lot; I spoke twenty-five hours with him. He's a nice guy. He was fascinated with the career of his daughter Paloma, a 12-year-old who is a kind of genius at classical dance and was chosen by Julio Bocca or by Baryshnikov to dance with the American Ballet Theater. I guess it was for that reason that he had developed a certain sensitivity toward child artists.

If he had declared that the paintings were the property of Julia Lublin, we would have had to prove that they were Guillermo's, something that would have been very difficult, because possession of movable property presumes ownership. My law office was certain that this was going to be his strategy, and for that reason we began to contact a lot of artists as witnesses to prove that in the art world paintings are often left in galleries without formal receipts, and that this had been the case between the gallery owner Julia Lublin and the painter Guillermo Kuitca.

We looked first for artists who had worked with Julia Lublin to declare to the judge whether the defendant signed or didn't sign consignation receipts each time they brought her a painting; all they had to do was tell the truth.

One painter who at first had accepted to be a witness later reneged because Julia had works belonging to him on consignment and she was selling them for him. We found out later that the works in question were drawings by Guillermo, which he had given to the artist a while back.

Another artist, who Jorge Helft contacted, also refused, declaring that in the past she had had a problem with Julia over some pictures; she had suffered a lot and didn't want to have to remember that moment again. Helft, who was dedicating all his energy to bringing the conflict to a satisfactory conclusion, took this refusal as a personal affront.

A majority of the artists didn't bother to look for excuses and when they were asked, just answered with an outright 'no.' Among those who offered to collaborate were Marcia Schvartz and Pablo Suárez.

The counteroffensive of Dr. Herrera and his client to the sequestration was way out of proportion. They presented all the plane tickets and receipts from trips that Julia Lublin had taken in recent years as expenses for representing Guillermo. Five star hotels, first class tickets on Swissair, etc. Even trips to art fairs at which Guillermo's work wasn't shown. The total was $ 80,000.

This move provoked a change in the original strategy; in the end we weren't going to need the collaboration of any artists as witnesses. What had to be proven now was not ownership of the works, but that Julia Lublin had not paid Guillermo for any of the works that she had sold to date.

To prove this point, we looked for help abroad: The Stedelijk Museum in Amsterdam and the Argentinean dealer Ana Jáuregui in Madrid presented evidence that Julia Lublin had collected monies for the sale of Guillermo's works, but she could not prove she had paid Guillermo his share.

The case got more and more complicated and, at long last, it was decided to start negotiating to try to reach an agreement between the disputing parties. Two years had gone by; we were all very tired now.

*   *   *

The first agreement we signed didn't work out. It had been agreed that Julia would keep all the paintings on consignment for twenty-four months, at a price agreed on by both sides, with a series of restrictive clauses that I had stipulated: The paintings could not be sold abroad, nor through another gallery; the works could not be sold at auction or all together; Julia could not use them in any publication with her name on it; she could not exhibit them in the case she opened a gallery; and she could not advertise them. Which is to say, just about the only thing she could do with the paintings was to sell them clandestinely. At the end of two years, works that had not been sold would be returned to me. I thought it was a good idea.

I was very nervous on the day we were to sign; it had been a long time since I had seen Julia and finally we were going to meet at my lawyers' office. By now, Agustín Zbar had taken over the case, because one day Rosenkrantz went to the United States on vacation and never turned up again.

The appointment was set for 7:00 in the afternoon but I arrived earlier; I had no idea how things were going to work out and, just in case, I dressed very elegantly.

At 7:00 on the dot the buzzer rang and there she was with her lawyer, Dr. Herrera. At that moment, I felt bewitched and realized that, in spite of all that had happened between us, Julia was still someone with whom I had a lot in common. We were both very nervous and I spoke to her spontaneously. 'It's great to see you!'

And instead of speaking directly to me, she said to her lawyer, 'He says it's great to see me.' But she smiled right away and we greeted each other affectionately.

This eased the tension a lot. Julia and I chatted a while about our different projects, and Dr. Herrera started to talk about his daughter, the dancer; he told us about how he had gone to New York to see her and he described the city to us; he was fascinated by the Metropolitan and with the hotel where he stayed. Then we signed the agreement.

But the problems weren't over. There was still the matter of insuring the works, and what was even more complicated, we had to put a price on each of them.

So, in a moment of weakness I let myself be convinced that we had to get this over with once and for all. According to Julia's and my lawyer, the only way to do this was to divide the paintings between us.

Agustín says that the second phase of the negotiations ended up like a bargaining session in a *shuk*. He and Dr. Herrera spoke on the phone at least three times a day. First they fought over the quantity, and then over the individual works, until they finally decided that Julia would get her choice of any four works with the exception of *La busca de la felicidad,* and we got the remaining twelve paintings. With that arrangement, we settled the suit out of court.

The pictures were finally taken out of the little room; they were intact. Julia took hers and sold them; mine are now stacked in my studio and I don't think I am going to do anything with them.

I know that Julia reopened her gallery; my lawyer told me. He received an invitation for the inauguration.

I saw her once again one midday. We ran into each other at a reception for the Juan Gris show at the Museum of Fine Arts. When we saw each other, we hugged effusively. Sonia, who was there, maliciously commented that it was obvious we knew we were being watched; in that way, we showed the world how well our relationship was and how much we continued to like each other.

One day Marcia Schvartz called me on the phone. She told me that Julia had asked her to exhibit in the gallery. Marcia said, 'Yes, sure, that's fine, but you've got to give me receipts, that's what Guillermo told me.'

'Take it easy, we're doing all the proper paperwork now,' Julia answered her. So Marcia decided to show with her and called to tell me about it.

'I just wanted you to know,' she said. 'What do you think?'

'Sounds fine to me,' I answered. 'It's a very good gallery.'

Bullewijk

I come home from work at dawn. In spite of my cap, my ears are frozen; it's December, but the canals haven't frozen over yet. They told me that some-times it doesn't get cold enough for the water to freeze until January or Febru-ary, and then something terrible happens: Everyone goes to work on skates.

I spent the whole night in Bullewijk and took the first subway back to Am-sterdam at around 6:00 in the morning. I am now at the stop waiting for the tram that will take me home and while I am standing there, a man, about fifty, with a blue and yellow Boca Juniors cap, approaches; those are the colors I've routed for in Argentina since I was a kid. The man is with someone else and they both stop to wait for the tram. They seem to be friends or colleagues, but they don't talk.

When the tram arrives, the two men take seats together. I sit behind them. They remain silent. I recognize from all the signs that we are approaching my stop, but I have already decided to stay on the tram. The companion of the man I am following gets off at the next stop. The two say goodbye with a nod of the head. Fifteen minutes later the man with the cap gets off at Central Station. There he takes a number 27 bus, which I also get onto. It skirts the port. It's a district with no houses, just warehouses and factory buildings, where I have never been before. I am surprised to see an enormous warehouse on my left; Lloyd Uruguay is written on its facade in large letters. The man gets off at the next stop. There's a snack bar. I go into it with him. We reach the counter at the same time and I hear him order a *frikadel* and two *kroketten*. I can't tell if he talks with a foreign accent or a local one. I order *broodje met haring,* trying to be as faithful as possible to the Dutch pronunciation; I am too far from home and way too tired to cope with people thinking I'm a foreigner as well. I sit near the man; he looks out the window as he eats. Then he leaves and walks a couple of blocks. He goes into a building that looks like a factory and doesn't come out again.

Cross Fire

A few months before I went to Holland, a political commentator began to appear on TV, and he became very popular. People told me that we looked alike, but at the moment I didn't pay much attention. And then a girl at a party grabbed me by the arm and began to shout, 'AAyyy, Marcelo Longobardi, Marcelo Longobardi, Ayyyyy!'

I was depressed for a whole week, but since I was about to go to Amsterdam, I got over it. I decided to let my beard grow and leave my hair long for my return.

But my stay in Holland lasted too long; instead of staying three months like I had planned, I stayed five. By the end of the first three, I had achieved my new look. But then I got tired of it and went back to looking like I did before.

Back in Buenos Aires, I was going home at about 2:00 in the morning, still with short hair and no beard, when some kids in a bar elbowed one and another when they saw me going by.

'Alex, Alex! Marcelo Longobardi! Look, Longobardi!'

They were saying it with conviction. The TV commentator still had his program, and his audience was growing by the day.

Depressed, instead of going home to sleep, I kept wandering around the city until about 4:30 in the morning.

That was my welcome home, besides the mail that had come, which was all for the friends who had stayed in my apartment during the time I was in Holland. Just two postcards came in my name; they were from them; on moving out they'd gone to Europe. For some, five months is too long, for others, too short.

But last Friday I went to a discotheque where a rock group was presenting its first record. At one point I went upstairs and installed myself in what had once been a box in the old-fashioned cinema that used to operate there before the place became a discotheque. My beard and my hair were growing but, in spite of that, a girl in a black dress and black hair, with her lips painted black, came over and asked me, 'Excuse me, aren't you Marcelo Longobardi?'

For an instant I didn't know how to react.

'Yes,' I said. 'Who are you?'

'Alicia. Are you really Longobardi?'

'No one but.'

Shocked, the girl remained silent. I looked at her hands; her nails were also painted black.

'I love Los Brujos,' I said to break the silence.

'Ay, I've never heard them.'

'Listen, come over to the studio tomorrow. Ask for me at the reception desk; tell the receptionist you're Alicia. The topic for the program is 'Today's Youth' and I'd like you to be on one of the panels. What do you do?'

'I'm a manicurist.'

'Great, I'll expect you to be on the program tomorrow. Don't let me down.'

When I went home I looked at myself in the mirror and promised to shave everyday, keep my hair short and only wear suits. Before everyone told me I looked like my mother; what I still don't understand is why no one tells her that she looks like Marcelo Longobardi. When I told her what was happening to me, her only comment was, 'It's a shame he's such a right-winger.'

Oh, Shoshana

One day someone named Susana called me.

'Hello, Guillermo, what's new? It's Susana. How are you? When are we going to see each other?'

'Uh, hello. How are you?' I answered, although I didn't have the faintest idea who was calling me; it has always been very difficult for me to tell people I don't recognize them.

Susana kept on talking and the situation became impossible, because she was really a stranger to me.

'Excuse me, Susana, but I don't know who you are,' I confessed.

'What? Don't you remember we met the other day in such and such a place and you gave me your number?'

I knew perfectly well that on such a day at such an hour I hadn't been in that place and I was getting more and more sure that I didn't know this Susana. So I told her, 'I do *not* know you,' and hung up.

From that day on Susana began to call every week. I think she was crazy so, in private, we decided to call her Shoshana. We repeated the same dialogue every time she called and I always ended up cutting her off with the same phrase: 'I do *not* know you.'

Her calls were becoming a habit.

'Didn't Shoshana call?' I'd ask the maid in the evening when I came home from the studio.

And Shoshana called more and more frequently, and she seemed so sure of herself that one day I wanted to discover more.

'What do I look like?' I asked her.

Her description was perfect; she knew my height, the color of my eyes, she knew how I cut my hair, what my next show was going to be, etcetera, etcetera. All the details coincided; it was obvious that someone had replaced me and, taking my place, had given all this information to Shoshana. I had a double.

I deduced that for Shoshana to be so obsessed, my double must be a much more fascinating person than I am, and I wanted to meet him.

'Shoshana, you didn't run across me this week, did you?' From that moment on, I began to ask her that question during every conversation.

'No, Guillermo, this week we didn't see each other,' she answered me.

'Then if we do meet next week, will you do me the favor of reminding me without fail to call home?'

But my double never called me.

Then one day Shoshana stopped calling. I think I ended up driving her crazy, if driving someone crazy who is crazy can restore her sanity. Or perhaps she finally got the real phone number of my double and now she calls him every week. Because I never again had news of Shoshana or of that other Guillermo Kuitca.

Aunt Berta

My Aunt Berta is a painter and she left some of her work in my studio because she didn't have any more room in her house, and I painted over one of her canvases, may God forgive me for this.

That painting came out well and ended up in Julia's gallery. On the back, written on each side of the stretcher, was Berta, Berta, Berta, and when Julia had to make the inventory of my paintings she still had for the law suit, she listed this one with the title, Bertas.

San Juan de la Cruz

That night Sonia and I went to look for Eduardo Lipschutz-Villa at the bar of the Plaza. Eduardo had come to Buenos Aires to get a small painting that Guillermo, who at that moment was in the southern part of the United States, had given to him.

In the restaurant, before they brought the order, a woman who was at the next table began to make eyes and wink at Eduardo; it looked like he wouldn't be able to resist her in spite of the fact that she was with her husband. This problem, together with that of the restaurant's prices, which weren't as inexpensive as Sonia and I had imagined, disrupted Eduardo's concentration on the points that we had to go over during our business discussion.

After dinner we were going to pass by Guillermo's studio to look for the painting because Eduardo was going to be leaving early the next morning. But there was another problem; Sonia hadn't brought the keys. In spite of the fact that it was almost midnight she decided to call Guillermo's mother, and the three of us took a cab to go and look for Mary's duplicate keys; it was a new set that had never been tried.

We took the same taxi to the studio, tried to open the door, but it wouldn't open. Then we all went to Sonia's to look for her set. I got out along the way; Sonia and Eduardo went on. And the cab driver.

Eduardo and the cabbie stayed in the taxi while Sonia got out to look for the keys. They drove back to the studio and, once there, paid the taxi. They opened the door and finally Eduardo could get his hands on the painting that had been the cause of so many comings and goings. It was a map on which many of the cities had the same name: San Juan de la Cruz. When they left the studio, each of them went their own way.

*   *   *

A couple of weeks later, Sonia took a taxi home and as she only had a big bill, she suggested going to the shop on the corner to change it. But the cabbie said to her, 'You have money, what does the change matter to you. You've traveled to Europe.'

'And how do you know all that?'

'I brought you to this same place not long ago, with some other people, a young guy and a bearded foreigner who spoke Spanish; he seemed like a Central American. And you talked about paintings. When you got out, the foreigner prayed.'

'What do you mean 'the foreigner prayed?'

'Yes, he just sat there in the cab praying...'

'Didn't he have a painting in his hands?'

'I'm telling you that his hands were busy praying.'

'Perhaps he was talking to himself. Did he have a rosary?'

'No.'

'Look, you must be confused, he must have been reading the painting...'

'No, no, no, we went to look for the painting later; he put his hands together and had his eyes closed.'

There was a moment of silence.

'Now, listen, don't ask me in what language... but he prayed until you came back. His hands were folded, he looked like he was in some kind of a trance, and the words he was whispering definitely sounded like a prayer.'

Morrissey

I've been feeling ill at ease these days. It's like I am going from one physical state to another. I keep thinking that it could be the end of my indecisiveness. I am afraid, for example, to look people in the eye. It's not that I can't, it's just that I don't.

One morning I made some coffee and it had a strange taste. I cleaned the coffee pot with vinegar but it didn't help. I couldn't recognize the taste. I, who have started to collect Italian coffee pots; I have seven, and the taste was the same in every one of them.

I had to meet a reporter in a bar that afternoon who was going to interview me for a teen magazine. I told him that he could recognize me from the photo on the dust cover of my book. I went with my mind made up that I wouldn't order coffee. We were both sitting there for over half an hour at different tables until we finally recognized each other because we were both looking around all the time. The reporter assured me that I didn't look the least bit like the photo on my book jacket; I felt a little embarrassed. That's when I realized that people who don't know me notice that I have changed; for those close to me I have stayed the same.

I had a dream that night. I was living in a satellite suburb and there was a commando group; its members were dressed in metallic suits. They appeared all of a sudden and they could make parts of people's bodies disappear with their weapons, leaving something black where these parts had once been.

I was witness to a commando attack against three men and a woman who were playing tennis. I was with some other people about a hundred yards but they didn't touch us. One simply had to go about one's life knowing that the commandos might attack at any moment.

The morning after the dream I stopped listening to my records. I also gave up going out, I worked at home, I cancelled my newspaper subscription, and kept away from the TV. Any music put me in a state of panic. The only thing that I could listen to was the Beatles, but only certain tunes. When I heard the first notes of 'For No One,' for example, I ran to change the song.

This morning, on waking, I felt better. I made a cup of mint tea (my publishers had sent me an ecological cookbook and I ate everything that it said to eat in the morning; the rest of the day I ate whatever I wanted). The mint tasted like mint and, as I was a bit happier, I convinced myself to try something that wasn't the Beatles. I picked 'Your Arsenal' but, just in case, I put the CD on 'random.'

The first song that appeared was the first on the record, 'You're Gonna Need Someone On Your Side'; what followed was the second, and so on until the end. Of all the thousands of possibilities, the 'random' mechanism had picked the same order for the songs as they appeared on the record. I was tempted to listen to 'Your Arsenal' over and over again and jot down the order in which the songs were played at 'random' to find a meaning for all this. But just as I decided not to start thinking about the universe or worrying about chance, I realized my CD had forgotten to program one of the songs, 'Tomorrow'.

Summerland

What detonated the war that summer happened when Crossato played tennis with Patricia Averbuj. It seems that at one point the little ball went over the fence and Crossato claimed he couldn't find it. The truth was he had hidden it.

Later that same day Patricia Averbuj went rowing on the artificial lake with Bengochea who, ever since he had arrived at the Grand Hotel, bragged about being a sportsman and how well he rowed; but Bengochea couldn't even get the boat off the dock and Patricia, furious, had to take over and do it all herself.

Mariana immediately sensed the strained atmosphere at the little bar in the Grand Hotel, a latent aggressiveness that wasn't there before. That night there had been open warfare – just a day before the barbecue that was being organized for Guillermo and Mariana. At first only one barbecue was planned. But now the group had split in two.

FIRST GROUP:
Patricia Averbuj (43)
Vivian (45) and her husband (42)
Daniel (38)
Eva Cziment (41)
SECOND GROUP:
The Crossatos (45)
Bengochea (42)
Bengochea's girlfriend (38)

It was the summer of '91. Overwhelmed by the heat in the city, Guillermo had set up shop in Mar del Sur with Mariana, his assistant, to prepare the second show for Annina. They rented a house on the beach and a couple of rooms for a studio in the Grand Hotel, where they were confronted by this strange atmosphere.

The people who spend their vacations there are mostly adults whose social relationships are in a state of exacerbation. One lives in constant fear of the danger of a never-ending conversation. At the beginning of the season everyone is friendly with everyone, but right away gangs, alliances, and competitive groups take form. The women go off and knit and the men play sports on their own. A bit intimidated by the mechanics of this tribute to communication, Guillermo and Mariana spent their days working, enclosed in the two rooms they used as a studio. Ahuva was commissioned to explain the multiplication of barbecues to them. The news annoyed Mariana.

'Mom, this is ridiculous. Just what are we playing, Camp Summerland? Don't you think they're all a bit old to be carrying on like this?'

Ahuva was too wrapped up in the situation to be able to answer. She spent the year making a frenetic campaign for Mar del Sur and its dilapidated Grand Hotel; she defended the place with tooth and nail. There were those who thought that she got a cut from Gamba for the guests she signed up in Buenos Aires. It was in her own interest and her family's that she keep the peace during these vacations. So when faced with the comments of her daughter, she limited her response to a gesture of indifference and turned around to go back to the Hotel.

The place that had been chosen for the two gatherings was the house on the beach that Guillermo and Mariana had rented, partly because they were the guests of honor – the arrival of an artist had caused a commotion in the community – and partly because it was neutral territory. So the two groups competed to see who could organize the better meal.

The first of the get-togethers was that of the Second Group and the chef was Bengochea. He prepared 'Chicken a la Vietnamese,' which left everyone drooling. No one could figure out how he could find sesame oil and fresh Chinese parsley in such a place. The evening developed pleasantly, but the prospect of stimulating conversation and of spending an unforgettable evening proved ineffectual. Perhaps that is why the night ended so abruptly, with a highly charged discussion about the Gulf War. Everyone was against Bengochea who, a bit drunk, defended a radical argument and didn't speak of anything except weapons and warfare.

The second round was for the First Group and that day Guillermo and Mariana couldn't work. They had been put in charge of selecting the wines and they spent the entire afternoon debating over the quality and quantity that they should buy. Bottles or jugs? They went to four or five local stores and they were tempted to go as far as Miramar, where they were sure to be offered a broader and better selection. They finally ended up in the shop of an old Brazilian where they spent hours deciding between Santa Ana and Santa Silvia. They arrived at the barbecue so late the guests had begun to wonder if the party had been postponed.

The meal, nevertheless, was excellent. They cooked different cuts of meat on the grill, from filet to flank steaks, ribs and rounds of beef. There were also beef sausages, blood sausages, plus all the innards, baked potatoes and yams, and a wide variety of salads. The meat was of prime quality and was perfectly grilled, the vegetables were garden fresh, from nearby farms, and no one seemed to pay much attention to the wine.

After dinner, the conversation dragged on eternally. It wasn't going anywhere. At the time, Vivian was the psychologist for the most popular South

American rock group, Soda Stereo. At first everyone expected her to liven up the evening with some juicy anecdotes, but she didn't. And since the party had to be a success, it was unthinkable for the guests to go home before 3:00 in the morning. So, at a certain moment, as if they were in an Antonioni movie, everyone went out into the garden to look at the stars, trying to recognize the constellations.

Ahuva was the only person who attended both parties. And that was why Mariana and Guillermo put her at the top of the list of candidates for 'Queen of the Sea 1991'.

*   *   *

The candidates for 'Queen of the Sea', besides Ahuva, were:
Mabel Dupond
Jackie
El Colorado (Red)
Viviana

Mabel Dupond
She is the wife of Gamba, the owner of the Grand Hotel. One day, since they couldn't have children, Gamba turned up with a blonde who gave him six or seven little blondes. Gamba eventually fell in love with the blonde, and he kept his real wife living all year-round in one of the hotel's miserable little apartments with an independent entrance which he calls 'bungalows'. Mabel lives there with her boyfriend Pedro and her mother Albertina, who reads palms. Pedro was a high-ranking candidate for the 'Best Dressed' award (blue jean mini-shorts without fringe that he wanders about in everyday); he also does maintenance for the hotel.

Gamba still uses Mabel a bit as a tourist attraction; he makes her sing in the dining room of the Grand Hotel where there is a show of sorts after dinner, like a cafe-concert.

Mabel's show always seems to be spontaneous and unrehearsed, although in reality everyone knows that she is going to sing and is waiting for it. For Mabel to sing, the audience must first perform a show of its own.

She appears with her dark, sultry look: short hair, eyes highlighted with Ultralash, and a black leather jacket and greets everyone she knows.

'Hello, Mabel,' the crowd responds. She waits a bit and then someone asks her to sing. At first she first says 'no, no no,' and then, when she accepts, she signals to Pedro with a nod. Pedro goes out and comes back with a tape recorder and a microphone which he always keeps in the room next door. He turns it on and begins to play a cassette on which all the music for the show is recorded. Mabel comes in from one side of the room, takes the microphone, and does karaoke. She becomes possessed and sings in French. She stands by the tables, leans on a chair and sings to one of the tourists. Her repertoire is straight Edith Piaf.

Mariana knows her quite well. She divorced recently and was feeling pretty tragic, so she immediately identified with Mabel Dupond. At one point she felt so sad that the girls (Ahuva, Patricia and Eva) took her in Patricia's Citroën to see Doña Vesela, an old Hungarian woman who lives way out in the countryside and sells wool. From there they went straight back to the hotel to knit. Mariana didn't like them taking so much care of her; she couldn't stand having them around, so she'd go off onto the balcony with Mabel Dupond and chat. Mabel's karma was the same as the karma of her songs; she was tragic, too. Mariana says that talking to Mabel was quite restful. She says she felt that they had a lot in common and Mabel made her feel less vulnerable.

Jackie
She was the second maid that Guillermo and Mariana had. According to Mariana she was named after Jackie Coogan. According to Guillermo, she was named Jackie because she looked just like Jacqueline Onassis.

El Colorado (Red)
One day Guillermo had gone to Mar del Plata. Mariana was alone that morning in the house and heard someone calling her. When she went out in her nightgown to see who it was, she saw a ragged man with a beard, red hair and a backpack. He said that Guillermo had told him that he was going to be in Mar del Sur and to come visit him. Mariana knew that the last thing Guillermo wanted was to have more people hanging around him. It was already enough with the Kinder Club from the Grand Hotel. But since she took an immediate liking to El Colorado, she told him to come in. His pack was full of compact discs and at 10:00 in the morning they were already listening to a Mahler symphony.

When Guillermo got back, he and Mariana started to talk in sign language to see how they could get rid of him without hurting his feelings.

That night El Colorado slept in the house and the next morning Mariana had been given the job of telling him to bathe. In the afternoon they went to the beach and he ate marijuana sitting in the sand; he opened his stash, chewed a while, and the effect lasted him all day.

And so, little by little, he went on winning them over.

That night Guillermo had a stomach ache, he was uncomfortable all over and couldn't hide it; but in spite of this El Colorado decided to be the host and took them to eat at Makarska. He ordered a plate that wasn't on the menu and gave the recipe to the waiter. It was during that dinner that he told them that when he did himself up as a transvestite he could pass for Rita Hayworth.

Viviana

One of the most critical problems in Mar del Sur was that there were no maids, so every time one appeared she was venerated. They had gotten Viviana through contacts; with Ahuva in the family nothing was impossible. When Viviana arrived, Guillermo and Mariana tried to make things easy for her. Even so they had to treat her like a friend to keep her coming. They bought all the brands of cleaning products she demanded and gave in to all her wishes. One day Viviana didn't turn up; Guillermo and Mariana waited and waited but she didn't appear. Finally Guillermo went to look for her with the car; she was in the middle of a game of Scrabble and couldn't be disturbed. There were days that Mariana and Guillermo waited hours and hours by the phone and they took turns going out onto the street just in case she called or appeared.

In the balloting, Viviana was elected 'Queen of the Sea 1991'. The voting was based on a point system and Mariana gave all of hers to her mother. But Guillermo went further by awarding the maximum number of points to Viviana. As the two of them were the only electors, Mariana had no choice but to accept the outcome.

Sandwich Days

'They're terrible days,' a friend told me.

He was referring to the days that were sandwiched between Rosh Hashana and Yom Kippur. Ponderous days, filled with reflection; terrible days. And since these days were terrible days for me, and the terrible occurred on the day of Rosh Hashana, I was inspired and decided for the first time to comply with the ritual of fasting on the Day of Pardon.

The only thing that terrified me was the idea of dying of thirst. They'd told me that the human body can go just forty-eight hours without liquids, and I was on the verge of spending twenty-four hours fasting. I had had a discussion with Guillermo. He said that one could drink fruit juices. I didn't know. I consulted with my other Jewish friends, but in our generation there was total ignorance. And I couldn't ask my relatives; I didn't want my parents to know anything about the fast. They weren't religious and I never had been; they wouldn't understand.

So that Sunday I decided to call a Catholic friend who lived in a Jewish neighborhood. I asked her to go down to the bakery and find out when the Day of Pardon started and what were the requirements for it.

'You have to stop eating and drinking when the first star appears on Tuesday and not start again until the first star on Wednesday evening,' my friend told me right off, without having to ask in the bakery.

In spite of the restriction on drinking, I decided to put my decision into practice. It was a very extreme measure, but I thought that by carrying the ritual to its final consequences, my situation might change.

On Monday I started to feel nervous. That morning I went to the supermarket and filled a cart. During the rest of the day I couldn't help stopping to buy something at every deli or market that I passed. At the last stop I bought half a dozen little meat pies, four cheese knishes, six spinach crullers, a loaf of rye bread and two pieces of zucchini quiche. Since I couldn't fit anything more into the fridge, I had to put these latest purchases in the oven.

It was finally Tuesday. I set the alarm clock to wake me up very early in the morning, aware that it was to be my last day for storing up. The first thing I did was to take a multivitamin pill and during the rest of the day I drank four two-quart bottles of mineral water. At 5:00 in the afternoon I put two breaded chicken cutlets in the oven. I realized that the first star wasn't scheduled to appear until 7:00, but I was afraid that for some reason they might not be cooked in time. They were ready at 5:25. I could have waited a bit and eaten them cold with mayonnaise, but my anxiety was greater than my capacity to reason and I devoured them in the act.

By 6:00 I had everything warming up on the stove. The moment was getting closer and closer, but I was still plagued with doubts. I didn't know, for example, if I could brush my teeth in the morning.

At 6:15 I spread everything out on the table, everything I'd bought, sweet and salty, hot and cold. I stuffed myself without stopping and I looked out the window during the entire dinner, my eyes glued to the sky.

And one minute after seven, when I saw the first star appear, full of relief, I stopped eating.

English Lessons

I am about to change galleries and Angela Westwater is going to call at any moment on the phone. I feel completely insecure. My relationship with Annina is fine and I have no idea what Angela can offer me. So I decide to take advantage of Finita's presence in Buenos Aires for a few months and I ask her to train me.

We spend two entire afternoons practicing questions and answers in English at her apartment on Tres Sargentos Street, but as I still don't feel ready, I jot the basic phrases down on a little piece of paper and make two more copies with the fax in the studio. Now I have the list of phrases in triplicate. I stick one on the wall by the telephone in the studio, another in my bedroom, and the third one is portable; I keep it in my pocket at all times.

Angela finally calls. But the dialogue never gets onto the subjects Finita trained me for, so I can't use the phrases.

Then, in a moment of silence, I say to myself, 'now or never,' and I begin to read from the paper.

'Well, you know, Angela, now, I've been thinking about your proposal of coming over. My concern is about you making such a long trip. What about if your terms don't meet my expectations? Now, on the other hand, it's exciting to think that they may meet.'

And I keep quiet; the next phrase doesn't fit at all and I don't even remember what it means; if I read it she may think I've gone crazy.

The result is that her answer is straight to the point.

'When are there flights to Buenos Aires?'

I look at the little sheet of paper and read: *'Tomorrow, 7:15 pm, United Airlines, checking in 2 hours before departure, you must be at JFK Airport at 5:15 pm.'*

Immediately after hanging up, I tear the sheet of paper with the phrases that's stuck to the studio wall into a thousand pieces. If she ever sees it, that's the end of my career. I decide, nevertheless, to carry the portable copy with me forever. Now that the transfer has taken place, I often talk to Angela on the phone.

House Plan with Raindrops

It was 10:30 on a Thursday night and Alejandro had been waiting for more than twenty minutes for his brother, José Luis, at the doorway of one of the tennis courts they'd built under the toll road. Since José Luis didn't come, Alejandro went into the locker room, hung his suit on a hanger, put on his shorts and, to save time, went to the counter to ask for a court.

'There's no reservation in the name of Lombardi,' the receptionist said.

Alejandro asked for the phone so he could make a call.

'There's a pay phone near the front door,' the receptionist said, and she pointed at it with a ballpoint pen she was using to finish a crossword puzzle.

Alejandro had tokens in his suit. He came back from the locker room and walked over to the telephone. It had a little sign that said 'Out of Order'. Outside, next to the glass door, a couple was fighting; a man about thirty, in a gray suit, and a girl who wasn't more than twenty-six, with a short white skirt, a blue t-shirt and a racquet. Alejandro also had his racquet in his hand.

The girl was making sweeping gestures and Alejandro could only hear her voice; the man was quieter and much more composed. He seemed to be trying to calm her down so she wouldn't start a row. But the girl shouted, 'Shut up!' and turned around and left.

Alejandro lost that night 6-3, 6-4, 6-2 to a stranger. When the match was over, he was in a really foul mood. He didn't like to lose and he didn't like strangers. He should have been playing that night with his brother, José Luis, who he almost always beat, in spite of the fact that he was his older brother.

In the locker room, Alejandro and the man hardly talked. They both showered; they both had everything they needed: soap, shampoo and deodorant. Then they changed into their street clothes. They were both going in the same direction and the man offered Alejandro a lift. He had a brand-new red Volkswagen Gazelle in the parking lot.

'You've got to improve your serve,' the man told him, once they were in the car.

'Yes,' Alejandro answered without looking at him.

They went down the dark streets of San Telmo and on one corner the car hit an enormous pothole. They both were jolted off the seat. Alejandro's head hit the roof.

'I've heard that there's one so big in Floresta, the neighbors put a washing machine in it so no one will fall in,' Alejandro said.

'I don't know Floresta.'

'Floresta, beyond Flores.'

'Yes, straight down Juan B. Justo, right?'

'There's one of the best steak houses in Buenos Aires there.'

'I haven't eaten since noon. Do you want to stop somewhere?'

Seated at the counter of a place where only cabbies were eating, Alejandro ate a flank steak sandwich and the man had one with filet. Parked between so many black and yellow cars, the red of the Volkswagen near the door appeared to glisten. The man talked about the blonde girl with whom he was to have played tennis that night. He met her almost two years ago. Every now and then she made one of these scenes, but she played pretty good tennis. Alejandro wasn't listening very carefully; he wasn't interested in the affairs of strangers. If he happened to be there at this moment it was only because he didn't want to mess up his brother's kitchen and he didn't like to go to restaurants at night by himself.

They finished eating and each one paid his share. Alejandro said that he was going to walk because he was staying close by. When they said goodbye, the man gave him his card:

Ruiz Núñez Inc.

Ricardo Ruiz Núñez, Associate Director

and told him that if someday he didn't have a tennis partner to call him. Alejandro put the card in his wallet, behind a picture of Jazmín, taken a year ago, pushing a red, white and blue plastic ball. He took out a card of his own and gave it to Ricardo. It said: García López Real Estate, Alejandro Lombardi, and had an address and three telephone numbers printed on it.

On reaching his brother's building, Alejandro didn't know whether to ring the bell or use the key he had been given when he moved in temporarily three weeks ago. He decided to ring the bell, which seemed to be the discreet thing to do.

'Did you forget your key?' Mariana asked him when she opened the door. She was his brother's wife. 'We left you some food in the kitchen.'

'Thanks, I already ate.'

'José Luis is in the computer room.'

The computer room was where Alejandro slept these days.

'He didn't go to the radio station?' Alejandro asked as he went down the hall, not waiting for Mariana's answer.

He went into the room. José Luis was staring at the screen. His face was green.

'How come you aren't at the radio station?' Alejandro asked.

'Today's Thursday, not Friday. Violeta called you about an hour ago. She wants you to call.'

Alejandro left the racquet and his bag on top of the bed but didn't say anything. José Luis insisted on teaching him to play Business Simulator and Alejandro finally relented. It was a game about high finances in which each player was the owner of a company for which he had to make a variety of decisions: how much to buy, how much to sell, at what price, and how much to invest in advertising; all this in the first stage. You had to enter the information on the computer to play. The machine processed everything and then made decisions.

Alejandro was sleepy but he couldn't refuse to play. He knew that, in any case, he wouldn't be able to sleep on account of the green light of the computer and the noise the machine made as it processed the information. Since he had moved to his brother's home, José Luis had already taught him the programs for three different games with such enthusiasm that Alejandro didn't have the courage to tell him he wasn't interested. In the first game he had to pilot a plane that flew along the east coast of the United States; Miami, Atlanta, Washington, New York, Boston. In another he had to handle public relations for a business in a variety of situations and with different people. And in a third he had to build three-dimensional figures that fled into the interior of the screen that got darker in little bits until it was finally pitch-black.

Alejandro managed to concentrate during the initial steps of Business Simulator. He imagined a business, it seemed foolproof, and he thought that it was a commercially viable project. But in just a few seconds the machine decided that his accounts were completely in the red and destroyed his illusion, and declared that he was bankrupt.

When they finished playing, about 1:00, left penniless and owing José Luis's company several million dollars, Alejandro remembered that he had to call Violeta. He dialed the number and waited as the phone rang four times. José Luis wanted to keep on playing; he was happy, he had finally found a game where he could beat his younger brother. Violeta's phone kept ringing and Alejandro was about to hang up when someone picked up the phone at the other end of the line, but no one spoke.

'Violeta?'

'It's Jazmín. Daddy?'

'Yes... no. It's Alex speaking. What are you doing awake at this hour?'

'The phone woke me up.'

Several months ago Jazmín had started to call him Daddy. That had been one of the reasons for Violeta and Alejandro's breakup.

'You should be in bed.'

'I was in bed. I got up to answer the telephone.'

'And Mommy?'

'I think she's asleep. Let me see... yes, she's asleep.'

'Javier too?'

'No. Mom is sleeping alone today. And you?'

'I am awake, talking to you on the phone. Now get into bed, it's already after 1:00.'

* * *

That night, Alejandro dreamt that his mother was telling him something that he no longer remembered: When he was very young, his family had lived in Mendoza, in two identical houses. They had gone back to Buenos Aires at Alejandro's initiative. In the dream, as his mother told him more details, Alejandro recovered his memory little by little. He asked his mother if the two houses were rectangular and if they were side by side on a plot without grass near the road, and if the facades were made of stucco and if they were smooth. His mother said yes. In the dream, instead of having a brother, Alejandro had a sister, just a year older than him, who had already travelled to Buenos Aires ahead of the rest of the family.

Alejandro woke up a few minutes before the alarm clock was set to go off. It was still dark outside. He took a sip of water from the glass he had placed on the desk before going to sleep. 'This must have been in 1969, when I was around two years old,' he thought, and then he realized that it had all been a dream.

He got up and went to the bathroom. Someone was in it. He went to the kitchen and sat down to have breakfast with his brother. He wanted to tell him what he had dreamt but decided to wait until José Luis finished his coffee because it seemed indiscreet to tell a dream to someone who wasn't wide awake yet.

'Have you seen anything lately?' José Luis asked him.

'Seen what?'

'Apartments.'

'Uf, millions.'

'For you, silly.'

Alejandro took the coffee pot off the flame and filled the three cups that were on the table.

'Not yet.' He opened the fridge door. 'Milk?'

'If there's none in the fridge, there isn't any. Maybe there's some cream left.'

It wasn't until much later, when he was showing an old apartment to a young couple, that he realized he had forgotten to tell the dream to José Luis, or perhaps that he hadn't wanted to tell him – he couldn't remember which – and now he couldn't remember what he had dreamt about either.

The apartment was on the ground floor and didn't have much light. The light bulbs were all burned out. He raised the blinds in the living room and in the dining room; these windows opened onto an attractive courtyard filled with plants. There were humidity stains on the walls; you could see that the house hadn't been lived in for a long time, although there were still some pieces of furniture. It was an apartment for someone to remodel.

When they got to the bedroom, the woman went to open the window, but she discovered that the window was sealed off with a wall of bricks.

'It's a bit claustrophobic,' she said. None of the three spoke.

'Yes.' Alejandro reacted after the pause. 'It's horrible. I don't understand how anyone would want to live in such a place.

*   *   *

When he got back to the office he found a note on his desk that said:

> *A girl called who's looking for a very large warehouse*
> *for artists to rent. Will you handle this?*
> *Sonia Becce 801-5462*
> *Silvana*

Silvana was a salesgirl at the real estate office. Alejandro looked around for her, but she wasn't at her desk. She was always referring the most absurd clients to him; because he was new to the job, Alejandro never protested. He was still holding the note between his fingers when Mrs. Perazzo, the employee who had worked the longest at García López Real Estate, came over and said, almost whispering, 'Lombardi, I've been wanting to ask you a question. My son-in-law brought me these cartons of Dunhill from the States and I don't smoke. By any chance, would you be interested in them?'

'How much do you want for them?'

'Twenty-five dollars a carton.'

'I'm interested, but I won't have any cash until the end of the month.'

'There's one carton that I've already opened for gifts. Three dollars a pack.'

'Have you got them here with you?'

Mrs. Perazzo nodded her head, affirming that she did.

'I'll buy two.'

The phone in the office rang. Alejandro waited to see if someone else would pick it up; Carlos didn't seem to be at all interested in answering it, García López had gone out and Mrs. Perazzo was too busy looking for the packs of cigarettes in a plastic bag she had taken out from under her desk. Silvana came out of the washroom and picked up the phone at her desk.

'For you, Alejandro, on two.'

Alejandro picked up the receiver.

'Mr. Lombardi?'

'That's right.'

'This is Sonia Becce. They told me you could help me.'

Alejandro looked at Silvana who was eating an apple she had just taken out of her handbag.

'I already told your colleague that the only time I'm free is after 8:30 at night and she told me that that wouldn't be a problem for you.'

Alejandro found himself forced to show Sonia Becce two warehouses for artists that very night, which was Friday. He opened a pack of Dunhill's but he realized he didn't have a light. He signalled Mrs. Perazzo, who was looking at him, with the cigarette. 'I-d-o-n-t-s-m-o-k-e', she mouthed.

'Sure,' Alejandro answered speaking softly. He had wanted to speak with his lips also, but he wasn't able to and his voice could be heard.

He decided to buy a lighter and, along with it, a candy bar. He could have lit the cigarette in the kitchen, but it bothered him to use the flame from the stove. When he got back, Mrs. Perazzo was holding the phone in her hand.

'Let me see, just a minute, here he comes. For you, Lombardi.'

'Hello?' Alejandro said.

'Mr. Lombardi?'

'That's right.'

'This is Graciela, Mr. Ruiz Núñez's new secretary.'

'Aha.'

'Mr. Ruiz Núñez gave me your card this morning...'

'Excuse me, Ruiz Núñez...'

'Ricardo Ruiz Núñez'

'Inc.,' Alejandro thought.

'And I wasn't sure whether to put you under Business or Personal.'

'Why don't you ask Mr. Ruiz Núñez?'

'Mr. Ruiz Núñez is in a very important meeting and asked not to be disturbed.'

'I understand. Put me under Sports,' Alejandro answered, and hung up.

*   *   *

It was 10:30 Friday night and José Luis was tired of waiting for his brother Alejandro at one of the tennis courts under the toll road. He had asked the receptionist who took reservations for the courts if he could make a call, but customers weren't allowed to use the phone, and the public phone outside the door still had a sign on it that said 'Out of Order'. So José Luis cancelled the court (to cancel the court you had to pay for all of the hours that had been reserved) and left with his bag and his racquet. He got into his car. It was too early to go to the radio station. He realized that for the first time since he had gotten married he had some free time that Mariana didn't know about. As he started the car, he thought he should be feeling some kind of excitement.

Like every other Friday night, the streets were full of people. José Luis drove aimlessly. All his friends were married. He turned on the radio to the station where he had his program. Magicians of Trash, Metal and Glamour still hadn't started; it was too early.

Even earlier, at about 8:00, on his way to the first of the warehouses, Alejandro had taken a bus and run into an ex-teammate he used to train with. The other guy started talking to him straight-away. Alejandro recognized him because the other guy was carrying a bag and wearing a shirt from the rugby team they had both played for, but he couldn't remember his name. He had been out of training since he married Violeta.

'I'm going to the club now, why don't you come and say hello to the guys?'

'I've got to work. Are there many left?'

'Not many. Gabriel Fuks went to live in Europe. I got on the team just after you left. You got married, didn't you? Several got married. It seems that Javier split up again. He hasn't come to practice for the last couple of weeks. He was living with Valeria for almost two years, but she went off with Julio Aguilera. And Javier went to live with that girl he had a child with back in high school. She left the guy she was married to for him. But Julio got tired of Valeria, and Valeria started calling Javier again. Then Javier left the girl he had the little girl with. Now they're together again, since the other day.'

Alejandro stood there looking at him in silence.

'Javier and Valeria. They're back together again,' he said.

Alejandro still didn't say anything. The other guy began to feel a little uncomfortable.

'It's like this, they got separated again and then they got together again, you follow?'

'Yes.'

'You do remember Javier, don't you?'

'Yes, sure.'

There was another silence even more uncomfortable than the first one. Alejandro felt responsible and said, 'But who did Julio leave Valeria for?'

'No one. He just wanted to be by himself. But now he's a wreck.'

'Poor Julio.'

'Yeah, poor guy.'

They both got off at the same stop. Alejandro had never felt less like seeing his old friends at the club again than now.

'So long, Alejandro.'

'So long.'

The warehouse was on a very dark street. On that block, there were two vacant lots on one side of the street and an abandoned factory building on the other. It was almost 9:00 and Alejandro had already waited for over a half an hour when a 1969 Renault Six stopped in front of him, just under the huge sign that said For Rent.

'I'm Sonia Becce. Are you Lombardi?'

'Alejandro Lombardi.'

'I'm late because I got lost.'

They went into the warehouse together. Alejandro tried the light switch to the left of the door, shoving it in the direction that was indicated on the card listing the property's specs, but no lights went on.

'It looks like all the light bulbs are burnt out,' Sonia said.

'In situations like this, you've got to find the main switch.'

He took the lighter out of his pocket and began to check out the walls of the building. Sonia followed closely, lighting the way with a little flashlight she carried in her bag.

'It mustn't be around here, I can't see anything.'

'The baseboards seem to be very interesting.'

They had gone all the way around the warehouse and were back again at the door.

'What kind of artists do you need a place for?'

'Visual artists,' Sonia answered.

'I'll read you the specs. It has over 8,000 square feet.'

'All without light.'

'It has light, it's just that I can't find the main switch.'

'Ah, you're right, that's what we were looking for.'

Alejandro illuminated Sonia's face with the lighter.

'I am trying to do my job the best I can. You are the one who insisted on coming here after 8:30.'

'I also told you I wanted the place to be within the city limits.'

'We are inside the city limits.'

'Does it have water?'

Alejandro looked at her without answering.

'I've never been so far away from downtown before.'

*   *   *

At the other end of the city, Alejandro's brother found himself following an orange Mercedes Benz which was going slowly down an avenue. The Mercedes blew its horn every so often at a girl waiting at a bus stop. Following this car seemed ridiculous, but José Luis didn't have anything better to do.

At one point in its journey, the Mercedes stopped and a very young girl, all made up and wearing a tight black skirt, went over to the window. After talking to the man for a while, she got into the car, but two blocks later she got out again.

A little later, the orange Mercedes stopped at a corner and a woman about forty-five with a suitcase and a child of nine or ten got into the car. José Luis followed them for a long time. At one point the child got out at a public phone and made a call. Then they drove through districts that José Luis didn't know until, all of a sudden, without knowing quite why, he realized that the Mercedes was trying to find the route that went to Mar del Plata.

While Alejandro and Sonia Becce were going to inspect the second warehouse, the 1969 Renault Six hit a pothole that was so deep it broke the steering
shaft. They were on a completely deserted street in an industrial part of the
city, though Sonia insisted they were in the suburbs. On that block there was
only one house with its lights on. Alejandro had gone across the street to ring
the bell, but the light went out immediately and no one came to open the door.
Sonia didn't dare to walk these streets by herself, nor did she intend to leave her
car completely abandoned in the pothole, and she didn't want to stay by herself
in the car while Alejandro looked for help. So they both sat in the front seat,
waiting for someone or something to get them out of this dead end street. Alejandro turned the radio on.

'Better leave it off,' Sonia told him.

'Don't you like Rata Blanca?'

'I don't know, I don't know them, but we're going to wear down the battery.'

'What do we want the battery for if we don't have the steering?'

Sonia didn't answer. The Rata Blanca song ended and they played one by
another local heavy metal group, Alakrán.

'I'm dying of hunger. I didn't eat anything all day.'

'I have a candy bar I bought this morning.'

'*Obrigado, não*. What is this? Can't we listen to something else?'

Alejandro didn't pay any attention. He had discovered a photo glued to the
outside of the glove compartment.

'Who's that?' he asked.

It was a person about forty with an orange tunic which came to his feet; he
had black hair and an Afro-type hairdo, and it was hard to tell if he was smiling
or not. Nor was it easy to make out if the figure was a man or woman. There
were flowers in the background.

'Sai Baba,' Sonia responded.

'It looks a lot like Cipe Lincovsky.'

'Ah, I don't know, I've never seen him.'

'A Jewish actress.'

'I don't think he's Jewish at all.'

'You are listening to Magicians of Trash, Metal and Glamour at 105.2 on
your dial on this Friday of the new moon, a dark and moonless night. Call us at
30-4250 and participate in our poll on Trash, the results up to now give 36 votes
for kidnappings, 44 for rapes and 56 for stealing tape recorders. Call us at 30-
4250. What do you want on a Friday night? We need your call.'

Sonia looked at Alejandro. Alejandro grinned.

'My brother has a program on this same station in half an hour.'

'Let's go,' Sonia said. They both opened the doors of the Renault at the same
time and got out. 'The last thing I need is to stay here sitting in this pothole in

some suburban street with this background music waiting for your brother's program to begin.'

They shut the doors and walked away on the cobblestones. Inside the car the radio was still going and it started playing something by Sepultura, a heavy-metal Brazilian group that, according to the announcer, was causing a sensation all over Europe.

*   *   *

At the radio station, the studio was still occupied by the Magicians of Trash. José Luis checked his notes, made sure his guest had been confirmed, and sat down to wait. His program consisted of an interview in which the audience could participate by phoning in. There was also a game taking place throughout the entire broadcast, but it wasn't always the same game. That night it consisted of trying to figure what criteria had been employed in selecting the songs that were being played on the program. He went over the list: 'Father Figure', by George Michael, 'Nos siguen pegando abajo', by Charly García, 'Bridge Over Troubled Water', by Simon & Garfunkel, 'Careless Whispers', by Wham, 'Aprendizaje', by Sui Generis, and 'Still Crazy After All These Years', by Paul Simon. It wasn't very tough. At the end of the program, the guest, if he wanted, could select and program three songs which, according to the circumstances, may or may not be a part of the contest.

*   *   *

Alejandro went back to his brother's with a bag from McDonald's. Mariana was in the living room listening to a song by Wham.

'Did you eat?' Alejandro asked her.

'Yes. Violeta called you. She said that she and Jazmín want to see you.'

'Sure you don't want a hamburger?'

'You didn't buy anything sweet?'

'A candy bar.'

'That's fine.'

He sat down to eat in the dining room. He had bought two hamburgers, two orders of French fries and two Cokes; he didn't need plates or silverware. The song by Wham had ended and he now heard his brother's voice and another voice he didn't know. He remembered Sonia Becce's Renault Six and he had an idea that they'd left the radio on in the car, tuned in to the same station. He imagined Sonia going back to that godforsaken spot with a tow truck, accompanied by a mechanic, and in the middle of all that blackness, the car still stuck in the pothole, she would be hearing the same voices on the car radio that he was listening to here in his brother's living room.

'I had a dream yesterday. It's odd that I can recall a dream, but every so often it happens, especially when I change my sleeping medication... I dreamt that I was with Barbra Streisand and we went to the theater together to see Barbra Streisand; there were two Barbra Streisands, a foreign and a domestic one. I was going with the Argentinean one to see the foreign one, but they were both exactly alike and one was just as good as the other. They never sang at the same time; before the American one went on stage, the Argentinean Barbra Streisand, who was with me, sang in the aisles. She sang exactly like the American and the audience applauded just as if she were the original. When she stopped, she sat down next to me because the show was about to begin. The theater was full of people and they did the human wave just like at the last World Cup, rippling rhythmically from the front of the theater all the way to the back. Barbra Streisand got up every time the wave came by. We couldn't stay for the American Barbra Streisand's show because we had to go to the country club where Lili Zac's family had a place. But when we got to Lili's family's place at the country club, Lili's brother-in-law told us, 'Damn, they should have told us that two more were coming, because there is no room.'

They began to play a song by Sui Generis, and almost at the same time the phone rang. Alejandro cleaned his hands off with a napkin and got up to answer.

'Hello?'

'Hello?'

'Jazmín?'

'Jazmín?'

Alejandro smiled and kept quiet for a second.

'Come on, Jazmín.'

'Come on, Jazmín.'

Alejandro blew into the phone.

At the other end someone blew too.

He whistled.

Someone whistled.

Alejandro noticed that Mariana was watching him, puzzled, as she ate the candy bar. Once again there was silence. He could hear the radio that was playing in both Violeta's home as well as at José Luis's. And the voice of Violeta above the radio, 'That's enough, Jazmín, let me talk now.'

'Tell your mom that I don't want to talk to her now.'

'Tell your mom that I don't want to talk to her now.'

Jazmín and Alejandro remained silent for a long time. The sound of the radio at Violeta's stopped. Neither of them said anything. Until Alejandro felt the pressure of the phone on his ear and said in a quiet voice, 'Sleep well.'

'Sleep well.'

And they both hung up.

✳   ✳   ✳

In his room Alejandro turned on the computer, ready to play Business Simulator. Mariana had fallen asleep on the sofa in the living room but the radio was still on.

'Have you chosen the music for us to listen to?'

'Three songs by Springsteen.'

'Bruce Springsteen and Barbra Streisand, they have the same initials in their names.'

'I hadn't noticed.'

'Why songs?'

'I once went to the hairdresser's and the woman who was washing my hair – she's always the same one – asked me if I ever repeat any of my paintings. I told her that it was something that you shouldn't do, but every now and then I couldn't avoid it and I did. "Sure, that's right," she said. "It's like singers; although they sing different songs, it always sounds like they're singing the same song." And that was how I came to do the series called Seven Last Songs. I wanted to get away from the idea of good and bad; even the worst singer has a voice you can recognize. I wanted to distinguish myself, but not for having talent, or intelligence, or some other virtue like that, but rather for something that goes beyond all that and is equivalent to what a voice is to a singer, like the hairdresser told me.'

Alejandro couldn't get the computer to work. The word Access was flashing on the screen. He had already pressed all the keys and wasn't able to get anything to happen.

'I like the idea of songs because in a song emotion is more concentrated.'

Now he had at least managed to do something: by pushing 'shift' and the e key, and one that said 'option', he had succeeded in getting the word 'access' off the screen, but in its place 'error' was now flashing.

'But the idea that they were the last...'

'In the beginning I numbered the pictures, but I soon realized that this was a mistake because there couldn't be a first last song, or a second, or a third... The only song that was really the last song was number seven.'

'That's logical,' Alejandro said. He turned off the computer and went to the kitchen. He put water on to boil and dropped a tea bag into a cup. The radio was playing music now.

The screen door slams
Mary's dress waves
Like a vision she dances across the porch
As the radio plays
Roy Orbison singing for the lonely

'Hey, that's me and I want you only, don't turn me home again, I just can't face myself alone,' Alejandro, who knew the lyrics, sang. He couldn't find sugar anywhere. He still hadn't discovered where everything was kept at his brother's.

In the living room, Mariana woke up and turned the radio down. Alejandro kept on singing, but after a few bars he realized this because he didn't remember the words to the next part of the song. Mariana came into the kitchen.

'Can I turn it a little louder?' Alejandro asked.

'I didn't know you were listening. Want some tea?'

'I was trying to make some. I can't find the sugar.'

'In the fridge, on account of the ants. Here, let me do it.'

Alejandro went into the living room and turned the volume up. The song had finished.

'One gets the impression that it is always the same house that you paint over and over again..., as if it was your own house.'

'It's a big temptation to relate the house plans to my own personal life. If I paint an Everyman's house plan it's because it is a long way from what I know; it's pure fantasy. The fantasy is not in the fact that something doesn't exist but that it does not exist in oneself. The world of the middle class for me is a world of fantasy.'

'Science fiction,' Alejandro said.

'What did you say?' Mariana asked him as she came into the living room with two cups of tea.

'No, nothing. I was talking to myself.'

'Sometimes when I hear José Luis, I forget he's on the radio and I get the impression that he's talking to himself.'

'That house plan you paint doesn't seem to be on a plot of land, or in a building. It isn't anywhere.'

'The idea of the house plans gave me the peace of mind to be able to use them as a method by which I could permit myself to forget everything else, as if there was something I'd inherited that assured me that everything was going to end well. Something like a background that was already resolved on which I could do whatever I wanted. I found the prototype in an issue of *El niño constructor* (The Child Builder).'

'I used to have *El niño constructor* when I was a kid. Is two enough?' Mariana asked Alejandro. 'A neighbor gave me almost the entire series. I think it was an encyclopedia for communist kids, or something like that.'

*   *   *

On Monday morning, Alejandro answered the first call of the week at the real estate office.

'I found a warehouse,' he heard someone say to him as soon as he picked up the receiver.

'Congratulations.'

'One was advertised in the newspaper yesterday, I rented it straight from the owner. But now I want to put my apartment on the market.'

'We would have to come by and appraise it.'

'Can you do it after 10:00?'

'We close at 8:00.'

'Then it's going to have to be early in the morning, like at 8:00. I'll be taking a Portuguese lesson, but it doesn't matter.'

'The office opens at 10:00.'

'I work then.'

'I also work then.'

'How about on the weekend?'

'Look, let me work on it, we have your number, we'll call you back.'

Alejandro hung up and went over to Mrs. Perazzo's desk. She was having breakfast, tea and biscuits.

'I want to make you a proposition,' Alejandro said quietly. 'I'll buy those cartons of Dunhill if you'll take care of a client for me.'

'There aren't any Dunhills left, but I still have some Camels. They're good too, very light, and they cost less. Twenty dollars a carton.'

'Two cartons?'

'OK, leave me the money and the info on the client in an envelope on top of my desk. I'll take care of it.'

*   *   *

Tuesday afternoon, Alejandro found himself an apartment for rent that he liked. His brother and Mariana's father put up the guarantees. It was two rooms in a high-rise in Palermo, almost brand-new. The ad in the paper said: 'For rent to foreigners'. The rent was high, but the place was just what he was looking for. From his apartment, 17 E, you could see several tennis courts which were right next to his building.

The next morning, Alejandro signed the lease and in the afternoon of the following day he sent over Antonia, the woman who did the cleaning at his brother's. Antonia waxed the wooden floor, cleaned the windows, polished the tiles and scraped off some decals from the opaque glass in the kitchen windows. Alejandro had hoped to move in over the weekend, but that same day García López made a special request.

'Sit down, Lombardi,' he said. 'I sent for you because of the Becce apartment. I want you to handle this sale personally. Mrs. Perazzo appraised it at $38,000. It's an apartment which has a young look, plants, pillows, paintings all over the place, you know, I think she's an art dealer. You're our youngest employee. Imagine Mrs. Perazzo in a situation like that. It would be ridiculous, don't you think?'

Alejandro decided to delay his plans to move. He had to be on hand at Becce's apartment Saturday and Sunday from 3:00 to 6:00 in the afternoon. It was Thursday and that night he went out to dinner with José Luis and Mariana. They were celebrating José Luis's birthday and Alejandro's move. They ordered a bottle of champagne.

'This is for you,' Mariana said, and she gave José Luis a little box with a new program for his computer. 'And this is for you.'

José Luis and Mariana's present for Alejandro was an espresso coffee machine like the ones in bars, but for making just one cup of espresso, and a set of ceramic ashtrays.

'For your new home. They say that a move is the third major cause for stress.'

Alejandro pretended to be nervous and nearly knocked over all the glasses on the table as he took out the present he had for José Luis: two cartons of cigarettes that he had bought from Mrs. Perazzo. When the waiter brought the first course, they had to remove all the boxes and wrapping paper that covered the table. They toasted; it was like Christmas.

*   *   *

The next day it didn't snow, but it was the coldest day of the season. It was almost the end of August, and by this time of year there was probably no one left in Buenos Aires who still believed in winter. But all of a sudden the thermometer fell thirty degrees, the sky was covered with clouds and by 4:00 in the afternoon it was already dark.

At 9:00, Alejandro and José Luis were playing tennis, like they did almost every Friday night, this time on one of the courts that was next to the building where Alejandro had rented his apartment. They had already been playing for an hour when a few drops of rain began to fall. Alejandro saw the little dark spots on the clay court's surface before he realized he was getting wet himself. His brother was about to serve and Alejandro pointed at the sky with his racket. José Luis served anyway and they kept on playing until they were both soaked.

In the locker room they decided not to change. The rain was so strong that once they got outside they would have gotten as soaked as they were already. José Luis had parked his car a few blocks away and Alejandro got the idea to seek refuge in his new apartment; that way, at the same time, José Luis could see it. They put their windbreakers on over their tennis clothes and ran.

The blinds were up and from the 17th floor you could see the entire city wrapped in an enormous cloud of water. Alejandro's apartment was completely empty and the only light fixture that had a bulb in it was on the balcony. It reflected on the freshly-polished wood. Alejandro and José Luis could see themselves mirrored in the floor. They took off their wet clothes, dried themselves with the towels they had in their bags and changed right there. José Luis tried to light up a Camel, but it was damp. He didn't understand why; he hadn't touched the pack of cigarettes and everything else in the bag was completely dry. Alejandro offered José Luis a Dunhill and they sat on the floor, leaning against a wall, waiting for the rain to stop. José Luis was next to the phone and he picked up the receiver to see if there was a tone.

'It works, even in this rain.'

'Give it to me. You reminded me that I have to call a client,' Alejandro said. He took his address book out of his pocket and dialed the number. No one answered for a long time.

'Sonia Becce? It's García López Real Estate.'

'It's Lombardi, isn't it?'

'Alejandro Lombardi. I'm calling to arrange to go to your apartment tomorrow.'

'Come before 2:00 pm.'

'But the ad says 3:00... From 3:00 to 6:00 pm.'

'I'm having my lesson then. Thank goodness you turned up again, Lombardi, that woman who came to appraise the apartment wanted to sell me contraband cigarettes.'

'You should have bought them, they're not expensive.'

'Tell me something, doesn't that woman teach aesthetics at the university?'

'Not that I know of.'

'Look, Lombardi, since it's you, now that I know you, I am going to leave the key with the neighbor in 6B. But you're going to have to ring the bell a long time, because sometimes she doesn't hear.'

*   *   *

It had stopped raining and the sky began clearing when the two brothers got into José Luis's car. Because of the cold and the rain, the motor didn't turn over right away. Alejandro sneezed.

'I think I caught a cold.'

'What do you expect, with a day like this... Today there's no program, the guys of Trash are going to broadcast the Rata Blanca concert live.'

'You don't have to go to the radio station?'

'I have the night off.'

Alejandro sneezed again. José Luis's car went down a street that gradually got more crowded with people. He turned to the left.

'I think that's a good apartment for you,' José Luis said, breaking the silence.

'I could really move tomorrow morning; I don't have much stuff to take.'

They turned again, this time to the right. The traffic light turned red.

'Do you feel all right?' Alejandro asked José Luis.

'Yes. Why?'

'Because I caught a cold, and since we both got wet, and we're brothers, were brought up together, ate the same food and all that... don't you think it would be logical for you to start sneezing, too?'

José Luis turned onto an avenue which was a bit better illuminated. Alejandro had no idea where they were going.

'I feel just fine.'

'Ah.'

They turned again, this time onto a narrow street and stopped on the corner at a red light, behind a metallic gray BMW; its left rear break light was broken and the car was so shiny it looked like it had never gotten wet. Alejandro had the impression that he had seen the car before, earlier that night. The gray car in front of them turned to the left and they also turned left.

103

'Aren't we going in the wrong direction?' Alejandro asked.

'The wrong direction to where?'

'To your place.'

'Ah, yes, that's correct. You're right,' José Luis answered.

And on the next corner they turned around, finally losing the metallic gray BMW that José Luis had been following all along.

The End

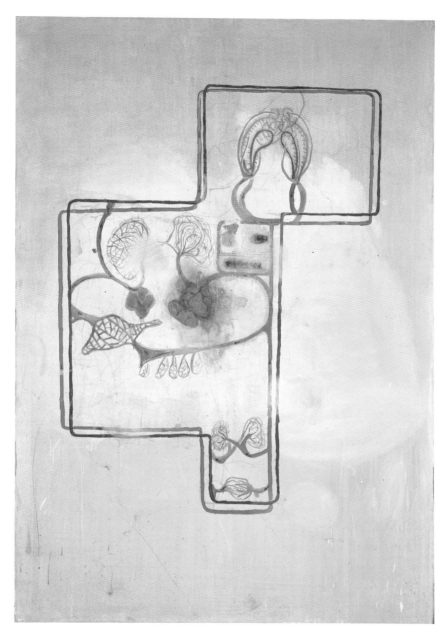

House Plan with Broken Heart, 1990
Acrylic on canvas
203 x 124 cm
Collection: Gian Enzo Sperone, Rome
Courtesy: Gian Enzo Sperone, Rome

Zaškov
Buki
Spola
Kamenka
Novomirgorod
NICA
Christinovka
Uman
Novoarchangel'sk
Tiškovka
Gajsin
Golovanesk
Nova Ukrainka
Pomošnaja
Pervomajsk
Blagodatnoje
Krivoje Ozero
Arbuz
Aleksandrovka
Domanevka
Slobodka
Balta
Kamenka
Troickoje
Voznesensk
Florešty
Rybnica
Veselinovo
Krasnyje
Okny
Širjajevo
Berezovka
Bel'cy
Lazovsk
Telenešty
Dubossary
Grigoriopol'
Kornešty
Kalaraš
Ungeny
KIŠINEV
Tiraspol'
Kamenka
ODESSA
ОДЕССА
Slobodzeja
Kotovsk
Husi
Bessarabka
Komrat
Tuzly
Kagul
Bolgrad

Odessa, 1987
Acrylic on canvas
125 × 88 cm
Collection: Stedelijk Museum,
Amsterdam

El mar dulce, 1986
Acrylic on canvas
180 × 280 cm
Collection: Stedelijk Museum,
Amsterdam

108

Nadie olvida nada, 1982
Acrylic on cardboard
24 x 30 cm
Collection of the artist
Courtesy: Sperone Westwater, NY

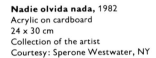

Nadie olvida nada, 1982
Acrylic on wood
140 x 50 cm
Collection: Private, Buenos Aires

Siete ultimas canciones, 1986
Acrylic and oil on canvas
207 x 200 cm
Collection: Alicia Taraciuk, Buenos
Aires

Siete ultimas canciones, 1986
Oil on canvas
131 x 201.9 cm
Collection: Angela Westwater, NY
Courtesy: Sperone Westwater, NY

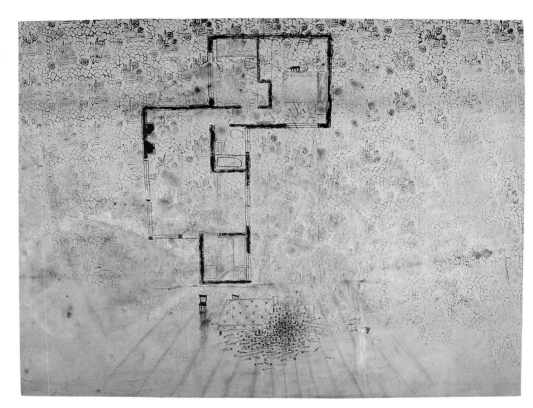

House with AIDS, 1987
Acrylic on canvas
157 x 214 cm
Collection: Marion and Jorge Helft,
Buenos Aires

Children's Corner, 1990
Acrylic on canvas
147.3 x 294.6 cm
Collection: PaineWebber Inc., NY
Courtesy: Sperone Westwater, NY

Gran escalera negra, 1988
Acrylic on canvas
160 x 225 cm
Collection: Marianne Cramer,
Warstein

112

The white plant was first and inside
the thought type plant
Convertible not to a diagram line, it
grows into volume — to once more
unroll the actual stories —family
— kids — chairs — no one will
perceive I am doing the same thing.

Work gets carried out amidst my personal
experience and the painting itself. I see not in
the terminated work — reality closeness moment is in greys. Degraded Impressionism
attends to form — be it a color painting photograph — it signifies not grey things. Family
situation: 2 rooms, 1 only son, a mother —
what I do not know: a son, a mother and a
father? — 2 sons not at home? 1 at home?
This house may be transparent, it has no door.
This painting one may not enter from above —
one may only see from above and there is
where the mirror appears.

Crystal glass separates
us from the house, we
may see how they live
but cannot live with
them, we may see how
they eat but cannot eat
with them.

Corona de espinas, 1989
Acrylic on canvas
179 x 123 cm
Collection: Peter and Maria Kellner,
London
Courtesy: Annina Nosei Gallery, NY

Plan with Text, 1990
Acrylic on canvas
135 x 97 cm
Collection of the artist
Courtesy: Sperone Westwater, NY

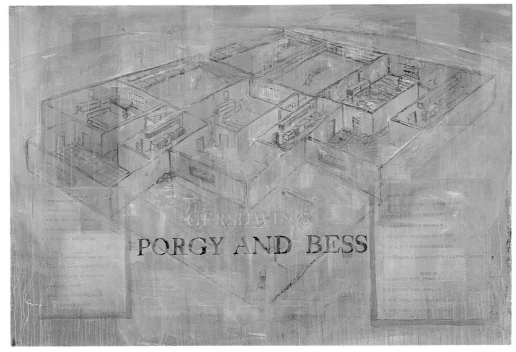

Porgy and Bess, 1988
Acrylic on canvas
160 x 225 cm
Collection: Stedelijk Museum,
Amsterdam

Strange Fruit, 1989
Acrylic on canvas
198 x 101 cm
Collection: Ingmar Pousette, Bromma
Courtesy: Annina Nosei Gallery, NY

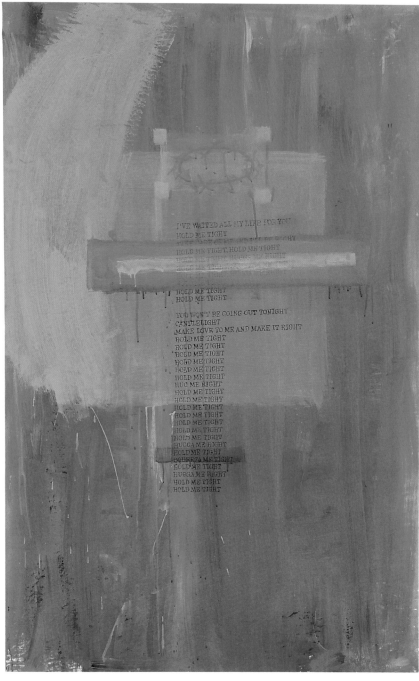

Hold Me Tight, 1988
Acrylic on canvas
140 x 90 cm
Collection: Mr. and Mrs. Lejeune,
Antwerp
Courtesy: Galerie Barbara Farber,
Amsterdam

Untitled, 1992
Mixed media on mattress
200 x 200 cm
Collection: Private, Caracas
Courtesy: Sperone Westwater, NY

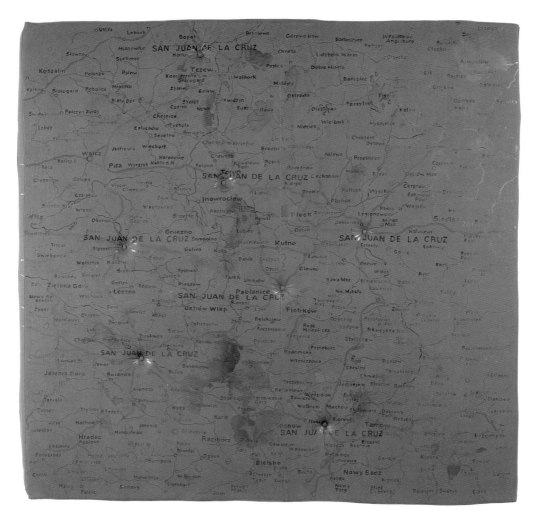

Untitled, 1992
Mixed media on mattress
200 x 200 cm
Collection: Sperone Westwater, NY
Courtesy: Sperone Westwater, NY

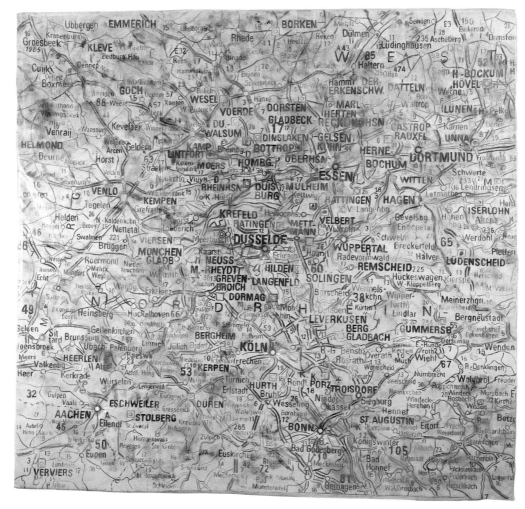

Nordrhein, 1992
Mixed media on mattress
200 x 200 cm
Collection: PaineWebber Inc., NY
Courtesy: Sperone Westwater, NY

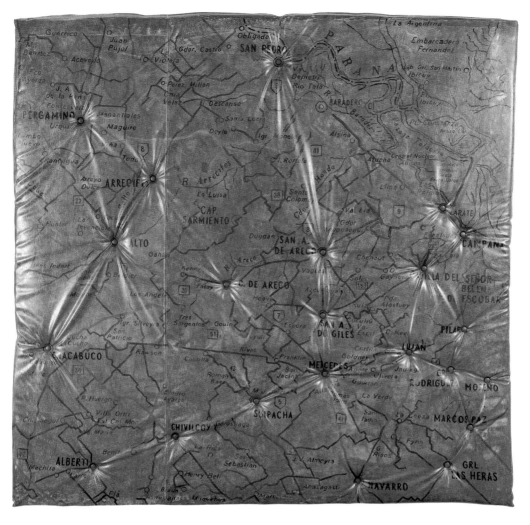

Untitled, 1992
Mixed media on mattress
200 x 200 cm
Collection: Sperone Westwater, NY
Courtesy: Sperone Westwater, NY

Untitled, 1989
(Diptych)
Mixed media on mattress
200 x 160 cm each part
Collection: IVAM Centro Julio
Gonzalez, Valencia

Jerry Saltz

Guillermo Kuitca's Human Touch

Guillermo Kuitca is a *painter of modern life*. He re-embeds modern life into modern art, but more than that, he is a painter of the pathos and the drama of modern life; the moments that define us, the touchstone times, the times we half remember and half forget, and all the misty stretches of oblivion that settle between our precious nebulous segmented memories. He paints the brooding moody shadow-play of life.

Inherent in Kuitca's luscious skittish paint, in every supple brushstroke is an elegant, subliminal sense of timing and an innate empathy for the moral and aesthetic issues of his time. When Kuitca paints a map, for example, his hand is never cold or stiff – it is charged with a deliriously focused veracity, a kind of inebriated control. Or when he paints an interior, he never loses himself in 'self-expression'. He's *very there* in his work, but he always leaves enough room for you. He's not some 'outsider' renegade, a Romantic with a mission, or provincial aberration – far from it.

His work and the issues he deals with connect up in extremely original ways with a number of other artists who came of age in Europe and America in the late 1970s and 1980s, although at thirty-two he is probably the youngest member of this group and the only one born and raised in Argentina. Maybe it's his age (in relation to these other artists) or maybe it's because he was so far away from the centers – but it seems as if he intentionally stepped aside and waited for the original tidal wave of painting that began in the eighties to pass – so he seems one (really good) step removed (rather than derivative or 'second generation'), or off slightly to the side of all the style wars of the eighties, and that makes him feel all the more real. It wasn't a 'strategy' so much as a natural occurrence.

In any event, it saved him from being lopped in with all the others, so he stands out that much more now. He's in syncopated time – in beat and in harmony – but he follows his own distinct melody. Music's not a bad way to understand much of Kuitca's work. Its pattern of repetition, the choruses, the rhythmic symmetry of form, the tonality and pictorial phrasing. Really you get the feeling that this is almost a *musician's* art as much as it is a painter's – and this keeps his work balmy and rich, makes it feel symphonic and large, not to mention pleasurable. Kuitca is a painter of the passing illusive moment, and even though some of the moments he paints passed a long time ago he gets these moments to reverberate with suggestions of something eternal and pervasive, cryptic and mythic.

If, as Baudelaire said, 'genius is nothing more or less than childhood retrieved at will,' then Guillermo Kuitca is possessed of this particular form of genius. Kuitca is a maker of maps, floor-plans and stage-like tableaux, who plots his diagrams within the intimate act of painting. His art is an act of retrieval that intentionally never quite achieves its goal and therefore remains locked in a poignant and powerful state of perpetual sorrow. This may serve to explain why he returns to certain subjects so often, why he uses and re-uses discrete props and objects the way he does. He's an insistent, even incessant artist who keeps returning to the scene of the crime, who is drawn inexorably to some primal source of memory.

His stage-set dramas often contain the images of chairs, walls, doors, stairs, pillars, wallpaper and beds. Indeed the bed is the constant in his work. It's been there since the very beginning (probably before the beginning). It's the Rosetta stone, his point of departure and the place he returns to most often. He's made paintings with beds, paintings of beds and paintings on beds. To understand this significance is to possess one of the skeleton keys to his chimerical work. It is the embryonic matrix of his work. Painting becomes a kind of *repetition compulsion* – something he's compelled to visit over and over again in an attempt to get it right, to load the painting with special feelings, to work as an undercover agent, an insider, an informant who is bent on telling a story, or getting information out. In this case the *out* is *in* – as *inside* the self; the secret places the id stores its recollections of youth or glory days of childhood traumas or times when the wild inner-life of adolescence rears its desirous head and triggers hidden needs and insatiable sensual feelings. It's almost as if he's paying *penance* for something, maybe someone else's acts, giving much of the work a delicate *sacrificial* scent. This also lends an unexpected operatic twist to his work – a *Der Ring Des Nibelungen* grandiosity that you get caught up in. But what makes Kuitca's art so special, so *cathartic* is that as personal as these things feel the memories he retrieves don't seem particular to him – they feel vaguely familiar, like you know what he's getting at. These are *big memories* not private masturbatory, autobiographical details. And you join his work the way you would in singing along with a song that has special significance for you. His art just *clicks* this way and it's moving too. It feels private and public at the same time, specific and general. His work has a knowing innocence – the residue of joy – in spite of all its shifting sorrow. There's something Kuitca is trying to share that many of us know – even if it's only on some instinctive or otherwise indistinct level. He's really trying to *atone* – not for himself – but for us all. And, again, you get this sweeping almost Wagnerian undertow. His is a sad, mournful art that positions the artist and the viewer on the outside looking in – lost in space (with the maps), above it all (with the maps and floor-plans), powerless and yet significantly, at the same time, *safe* out of harm's way.

Kuitca paints not only a world (the repetition breeds familiarity) but a *world view*. You enter his world completely and it envelops you. It is a world of complex emotions, elliptical afterthoughts and quicksilver perishable space, a work where evasiveness holds sway. Things drift in and out of consciousness and no single definition will do, and like the song you sing along with, you look at a Kuitca painting over and over again and each time a slightly different meaning or emotion filters through while at the same time it remains the same.

His paint is visceral and juicy. It's as if he's mixed in an elixir or an aphrodisiac into it. The surfaces are sensuous and alive. You want to touch them when no one's around. They almost seem to have a pulse. There's something incredibly human about them. They radiate a flower-like or jewel-like energy. They tend to take up a lot of psychic space. They're about *big problems* – bigger than you or me – and this endears them to you. They're generous. It's like they're trying to do something *for* you and not just to you.

His 'big' themes are not unusual: the vulnerability of childhood (the stage sets), the conflicted feelings of adolescence (the apartment floor-plans) and the gross power of nationhood (the maps) – but his methods are a blend of familiar and mundane forms which the artist combines in extremely evocative ways. As an artist, Kuitca himself may be said to be on the outside looking in: A participant in the European tradition of painting without being completely a part of that tradition. Although he is from South America, his paintings don't feel especially South American (whatever that might be) and this foils the 'multi-culturalists'. They can't claim him as one of their own. Maybe it's because of the peculiar history of Buenos Aires that Kuitca is more than a 'third world artist' (indeed this term has a disturbingly elitist ring about it – as if any artist other than an American or European might fall under this dubious rubric and thus not be taken seriously).

Kuitca draws on conventions of Abstract Expressionism, Neo-Expressionism and (surprisingly) New Image Painting. (Consider the dual facts of his being only seventeen years old when New Image Painting was attempting to reinsert representation into painting, and that New Image Painting was so completely eclipsed by Neo-Expressionism when it came along in around 1979 that many of its possibilities were never really followed up on by younger artists.) He melds these three 'isms' into a distinctively original visual style whose subject is power viewed from a position of (relative) powerlessness. In other words Kuitca, like most original artists, is an anomaly while being utterly a product of his own time.

There's an incredible ebb and flow to Kuitca's work. And because he's from Buenos Aires it would be tempting to compare him to the erotic rhythms of the tango. He's really more like a waltz – or better yet, a waltz with the musky scent of the tango. He zeros in and then pulls silently away, approaching and reproaching, finding one thing then looking for another. All of this reveals an intensely conceptual underpinning that carries the work along. All of Kuitca's work is an act of reclamation, a search for the truth, and simultaneously an act of *redemption*.

Tracking Kuitca's development is like entering a maze where things are familiar and yet unpredictable, where the plot line is revealed slowly, without fanfare, through derivation and permutation. You accept Kuitca's world unconsciously, almost by accident, so structured and 'logical' is it. It starts to make sense. You learn its rules and regulations, its grammar and syntax as if by osmosis. But as organized as the paintings are, as when we instantly recognize his apartment floor-plan, they're fictions that masquerade as facts, parts that seem whole. The paint always feels fresh even though he often works in sullen tertiary tones. Nevertheless, there's a dreamy veracity to Kuitca's universe of pain, sorrow, suffering, play and movement that makes you have faith in the story he's telling. Not to make too much of it, but many of the paintings have the ring of Bible stories: tales of miracles and extraordinary events set in the everyday world. His is a spirit-vampire world peopled with the shades of all our unexpressed emotions and unsung wishes. They're wishing wells. In the end, these paintings open up to reveal a world of oceanic insight, mystery and endless tenderness. His touch is sumptuous and full, warm and subtle. It's a child's touch but with the mind of an adult. Kuitca's heart feels young but his soul feels old.

Essentially, Kuitca's work can be broken down into three or four loose categories that progress from the early eighties (when Kuitca was barely out of his teens) to when he began by making simple paintings of props; beds, lamps, tables, chairs and ghost-like figures set in fields of undifferentiated monochromatic paint. These are the most fragmentary of all Kuitca's work and they signal him as 'setting the stage' as it were, determining the basic players and props of the drama that was to unfold shortly. They're like premonitions from the vast sea of oblivion. The things in the paintings seem burned out from exhaustion, and weirdly ravaged – looking for a place to rest. These are a preamble to Kuitca's more mature work. Even so, they have a well-developed sense of space and formal placement and they already belie that unique way he has with *isolation* and *aloneness*.

Things float in gravity-less non-space. These are images deprived of time and place and of the light of day. They're very artificial this way, almost pictures of imaginary prison-cellular space. They're filled with protean scrapes of protoplasmic memory and imagination. They feel cut-off, inconsolable and a little doomed. But they have that naive, child-like touch, a whimsy that will run through much of his subsequent work. These paintings produce the same dread that feeling around in the dark does – there's something blind and groping about them, something half-seen. These are the images that feel the most like a child's memory of the world; incredibly piecemeal and eternally incomplete. There's a smallness about this – almost underwater – world. They're very short stories – short-lived flashes – fissures of memory that close even as they open. These are the most private of all of Kuitca's work – the ones we can know the least about. They are absurdly simple odes and one note songs – like humming.

Guillermo Kuitca built out from these humble visionary beginnings and slowly this single note sprang into something symphonic. By 1985 it is clear that Kuitca's mind is at least *operatic*. These paintings which mark the second stage of his development but his first 'important' phase are wet-on-wet imaginary stage-sets peopled with sitting, lying, lounging and standing figures, more furniture and space. Not quite real space, but a witchy implied space, as if the dreamer is in a more active state of sleep. Lines proceed back into murky distant space or terminate in shadowy factories and apartment buildings. There's a weird outdoor feel to these paintings as if the things in them were exposed to wintry elements. There's a concentration-camp chill that haunts the work, even though they're enclosed 'pretend' places: not quite nightmare spaces – but close.

Kuitca has introduced space but he's left out time. This is Ur-time: now and not-now, then and soon – and this causes the work to have a wonderfully woozy intoxicated surreal-ness to them (but they're still rooted in fiction, as the events are fairly strange and splintered. The paintings are Gothic this way, very Mary Shelley.) You reach for them – mentally – but you can't quite grasp them. You don't know how you got here exactly. And you're not sure if this is a world with or without prospects and this is kind of creepy. They're melodramas lit by mechanical spotlights. The action is reduced and disjointed and in herky-jerky motion. In one, *La Buenos Aires-Wuppertal* (a title which already hints at a traveling motif that will be picked up in earnest) three women sit on a couch (there's a lot of languid waiting around in this phase of Kuitca's work, as if the people he depicts lack the necessary will to move) while a man in a striped robe stands inexplicably on a chair, looking off into the De Chirico-like fantasy city in the background, while stairs lead out of the picture. Everyone's so out-of-energy – almost skeletonless. Figures are strewn and sprawled haphazardly in the background suggesting violence and silence.

In another painting a Dickensian drama unfolds within a sunless interior. A figure silently carries another limp figure into the background of the painting while a white cross burns its way onto the wall. Its title *Si yo fuera el invierno mismo (If I were Winter Itself)* is pretty sensational and marks the artist placing himself well within these horror stories. They read a little like murder mysteries and they show Kuitca combining a number of influences in unique ways.

On one hand these works hark back to a strain of post-minimalism in America known as 'Story Art' (which was practiced by such artists as Terry Allen, Ida Applebroog, Alexis Smith, William Beckley, Eleanor Antin and, to a certain extent, Laurie Anderson). Story Art, and for that matter much art of the late seventies, sought to reintroduce narrative and content into painting. Indeed, Performance Art was singularly obsessed with this end, and it should be kept in mind how influential Performance Art was on a young generation, and how Kuitca's art is so predisposed toward theatricality. But where the art of the seventies was surreptitious about it – trying to sneak content back into the House of Art – Kuitca brought a much more unabashed eighties – Schnabel-like – sensibility to it, he wasn't subtle about it. It's hard to remember now just how 'off limits' content was, and how difficult it was to find ways to make paintings 'interesting' again. Kuitca, though young at the time, was one of those artists.

In this period of his work, Kuitca paints a world where dark forces dominate. In another work from 1985, *Vaga idea de una pasion (A Vague Idea of a Passion,* a recurrent title) another starless interior is depicted – only now two nearly naked figures droop over the tables, while another figure lurks behind a half-opened curtain. A miniature house sits on the floor as a dog and cat look on. The walls are lined with wallpaper emblazoned with the letter *K* (we assume for Kuitca, who again is finding ways to interpose himself in the narrative. This is similar to the way Jorg Immendorff placed himself in his Cafe Deutschland paintings.)

By 1985, of course, German, Italian and American Neo-Expressionism was well established. It's not that Kuitca was directly influenced by any artists or movement, rather it's as if Kuitca stepped deftly aside, like a matador, and let this rampaging bull pass by, then when he was safe from being branded as a 'follower' he invented his own brand of painterly expressionism. It's amazing because it was against all odds. Most painters got swept aside or were drowned in the undertow. Kuitca, perhaps unconsciously, took the best parts of local pictorial tradition (a tradition that most Europeans and Americans were unable to tap); magic realism, images of the fantastic and pictorial paradox – but he groomed out a dangerous strain of Surrealism that poisoned much South American art. He also abandoned an obsessive realist verisimilitude endemic to Latin American art. In place of these he added his own version of a more universal story. And in so doing, Kuitca became the first contemporary artist from South America to distill all these influences flowing in from the outside while combining it with something unique to Latin American art.

Now, in turn, Kuitca has influenced the 'outside'. In effect, Kuitca finally completed the cycle.

These stories soon grew into *Passion Plays* as a drama larger than Kuitca's own personal narrative was being played out. The Passion historically is a record of the last events of Christ's life from His entry into Jerusalem to His burial. Kuitca de-religionizes The Passion and transmutes it into a secular Passion, a sort of *Every Passion*. As early as 1984, in *El Mar Dulce (The Sweet Sea)*, Kuitca employs a cinematic jump-cut technique depicting a multiplicity of actions: a film still of Sergei Eisenstein's famous Odessa staircase scene from the film *Potemkin*, in which a baby carriage tumbles down a staircase littered with murdered babies (itself a secular allusion to *The Massacre of the Innocents*); a couple having sex; three naked figures with their backs turned to you while peering into a mirror; a seated figure with another person kneeling at their feet. The simultaneity also echoes techniques used in Medieval art. Kuitca's Passion is one of potent individual dramas – they aren't the same as, say, The Last Supper or The Agony in the Garden, but they do feel packed with unspecified symbolism.

But by 1986, the action was simplified even more as something starkly coded and deeply human filters to the surface. In a work like *Siete últimas canciones (Seven Last Songs)*, a beautiful and quasi-religious sounding title (Kuitca's good with titles – they sound sort of sacred without being ridiculous or heavy-handed), a hush falls over the painted stage, and the stage itself is transformed into a more mythic, less specific setting. A greatly elongated bed dominates the foreground. Near it the baby carriage from the Odessa staircase scene begins to fall into a hole in the floor, while a little naked figure droops over in a chair. In the barren background, a microphone stands in a spotlight, and two blackened doorways accent the checker-papered wall. Here a quiet has descended over the work and a secluded mystery overtakes the space. There's a ritual air about Kuitca's paintings, as if the events in them happen over and over again. This gives them a subtly tragic side.

In a tragedy we see a character heading to his or her fate and we are helpless to stop them. No matter how many times we read the story of Oedipus, no matter how many times he's warned of his impending doom, he proceeds headlong into it. The same is true in Kuitca's work. But you don't know who the person is you should be trying to warn. Is it Kuitca or you or everyone or no one? Whoever it is you want to cry out. Some of the paintings from this period read a little like *retablos* – small votive paintings that offer thanks to a holy being (usually The Virgin) for misfortunes escaped. These works (which are also called ex-voto paintings) depict both the event and the holy agent of miraculous salvation. This is also the Latin American side to his work, or rather it is the DNA that runs through it. Usually, when an American or European tries his hand at this the results are labored and didactic. It never rings true. This kind of 'miracle painting' must run in Kuitca's blood.

In *Siete últimas canciones,* we witness an event, or the figment of an event, but mostly we witness the aftermath. We're also keenly aware that Kuitca has transformed looking into witnessing. His sense of timing is impeccable. It's one of the keys to his otherwise hermetic work. There's always a feeling of having arrived just after something's happened (or like a homicide detective arriving at the scene of the crime). You missed something. You're too late. Thus a sad feeling or a sense of guilt accompanies looking at much of Kuitca's work of this period. You want to have burst in in the nick of time – but you never do – Kuitca never allows this. In this way, his work is taciturn and a little aloof. He stands back and repeats the drama over and over. You want to stop it but you can't. And after a while you become a little addicted to this strange visual-emotional sensation. Kuitca's work often involves the same aesthetic faculties as theater or poetry. It's not that he's trying to make plays (a lot of writers have him following in the footsteps of Pina Bausch). He's not a follower of Bausch. They came to similar conclusions in the mid-1980s, that's all. The air in Kuitca's paintings is dense and lurid, filled with ectoplasm. Something important took place here but we can't say just what it was. All this gives his work a special hallucinatory side. It lets you see a little into the past – only an instant – but a powerful epiphany forms around this instant. 1985-1986 finds Kuitca, who was by then twenty-five years old, at the end of the first complete phase of his work and on the threshold of his full powers as a painter.

In 1986-1987, the dam of Kuitca's creative powers finally gave way and poured forth new idea after new idea. The bed, which Kuitca placed at the forefront of so many of his past paintings, now emerges as a kind of vessel – a magic carpet or, more accurately, a life raft and a shelter from the storm. It is a place of sex and dying, dreaming, fantasy, escape and deliverance – a place from which Kuitca takes on the world. It's a life buoy: the quintessential carrier of the spirit and the flesh. Here Kuitca is like Ishmael (from *Moby Dick*) – an archetypical *sole survivor* of some unnamed (and unnameable) cataclysm. The Ishmael reference is of further interest as Kuitca never portrays himself as a hero, or someone to be admired. It's almost as if he's here by *divine providence* (which is a little more than lucky, but less than 'chosen'). Rather, Kuitca serves as a signpost or a warning or an example. He's in a state of perpetual exile – a refugee, an orphan in the storm, an emotional expatriate – but he's in *a state of grace*. Dorothy in *The Wizard of Oz* spiraled into another kingdom in her bed. And *Papillon,* the convict sentenced to life imprisonment on Devil's Island, the French penal colony located off the shore of French Guyana in 1973, wrote how he'd lie in his bed, wrap his head in a towel and 'travel' all over the world from his solitary cell. This is the kind of mad mental travel that the bed represents for Kuitca. He uses it to talk about danger and isolation, catastrophe and abandonment in a touchingly childlike voice – but a voice that is gently tinged with horror. This bed-as-life-raft conjures the image of other rafts and crafts from history and imagination. Delacroix's *Bark of Dante* where we see Dante and Virgil crossing the infernal river Styx over the ruined and tormented souls of the vanquished, guided by the monstrous ferryman Charon. Or perhaps Gericault's *Raft of the Medusa* – that floating plane of resignation and apprehension, desire and death. All the images of the excluded, the deserted and the outcast come drifting in from the far reaches of the earth. Of Ishmael (again) on Queequeg's coffin-like raft floating alone after the maelstrom, awaiting rescue, Gulliver shipwrecked in the lands of the large and the small. Tarzan marooned and incarcerated in the mentality of an animal. Of Jonah thrown overboard by his wary shipmates and on his way into the belly of the whale speeding toward him. Of an empty ship infested with plague, drifting into the lagoon of Venice. The lifeboats of the Titanic weighed down with already dead caste systems. Of forgotten pilots floating on rubber rafts, only to be eaten alive by sharks. An oceanliner filled with Jews escaping Nazi Germany, only to be turned away by Cuba and the United States and back to their certain annihilation. Of Huckleberry Finn's drifting nomadic journey down the long-winding heart of America. We are haunted by Kuitca's little bed. This bed was about to metamorphose into new forms. Its innocence, once so bright is now the color of quarantine and pestilence, of imprisonment and seizure. It's silent now like some Alamo, a shrine to what once was; of heroes and battles gone by. And this is its hope – that it looks back. That it miraculously seems to have survived. It looks back in anger, frustration, pride, rage and sorrow to an astonishing struggle. This homeless bed is a symbol not only of the confinement of the lost but of the salvation and deliverance of all who would ride out the storm.

Two new things appear in around 1987 that would be the thrust of much of Kuitca's work thereafter: the map and the floor-plan of an apartment. By 1989, this apartment would be codified into a standardized layout – a modest two-bedroom quasi-middle class urban apartment which Kuitca would render in a myriad of situations and styles (a whole exhibition of these so-called 'floor-plan paintings' would make for an extraordinary show in and of themselves). It was as if Kuitca eliminated everything but the abstracted signifier of the apartment (which is a vaguely oblong cross-shape) as the site of all domestic – and therefore all formative – dramas.

Often these floor-plans hover mysteriously in empty monochromatic voids, pockmarked and marred with pediment, as if tattoos or architectonic stigmatas. They're like icons. An early 1988 pre-standardized version titled *Planta genela* has a hole cut out of its center as if to suggest loss and mourning. So you know Kuitca wants to use this geometric form in a symbolic manner. He's (obviously) not Neo-Geo but he does push abstraction toward meaning and away from purity. This plan with the hole cut out is reminiscent of being in a house after a lover leaves – how their presence hangs in the house, sometimes for years. How, when you walk through certain rooms you remember things you did with them there. How your private memories are there all the time – existing like a ghost alongside the mundane reality that your friends and neighbors see. The painting is a reminder too of how weird and embarrassing it can be to have someone new into your home – like maybe they'll catch a glimpse of this otherwise private invisible side of your past life. Kuitca's paintings want to know how long a memory haunts a house. He finds a way to address that phenomenon of the private and the public. His work opens up the issue of each one of us having two lives. One, the open life everyone knows about – your public life – but the other is the private life only you and a few people you've shared it with know about. The private times when you're the most you. You share these times with certain friends and lovers – but mostly lovers. The good times, bad times, wild times and wicked times – moments of intense pain and pleasure. Times when you're alone and filled with desire, haywire with passion – looking for love or sex or whatever – times filled with private thoughts and secret fantasies that only you know about. The things you and that other person take to your graves. These people we loved and were loved by are our biographies – who we really are. These people are places, are markers, the brief respites from our 'regular, normal lives' – the times when hunger and pleasure prevail, when heat wins out over reason and fear – when urge is more important than duty. Times when you get away from yourself *to yourself*. Every part of our bodies contains memory. Proust said 'our arms and legs are full of torpid memories.' Guillermo Kuitca makes these apartment plans turn into those memories.

In another painting titled *House with AIDS,* the floor-plan is superimposed over a decorative wallpaper pattern, while a bed, chairs and flowers are strewn below. The painting is like a *memento mori.* These early plans were like maps and diagrams of scenes. They had the architectural notations for windows and doors. But by late 1988 the door disappears and you realize that this place is truly not physical but *metaphysical.*

Taking away the door is important and it has been overlooked until this point. Its significance can be illustrated by a painting Botticelli made very late in his life of a man sitting slumped over, just outside a narrow doorway. In this case, the door has no doorknob. To understand the meaning of this it might be useful to recall that, according to Dante, the Gate of Hell had no door. It was merely an open maw which anyone could stumble into. Not so the Gate of Heaven, which according to legend is a small doorway, with a plain door that has no doorknob. The symbolism is clear. The Gate of Heaven *must* be opened from the inside while the Gate of Hell is always open. Kuitca strikes a kind of Purgatory middle ground. In removing the door, we understand that the only way in or out of these 'apartments' is through the *inner doors* of imagining or remembering – through consciousness. Little things mean a lot to Kuitca. So taking the doorway out of the plans is no coincidence.

In *Coming* from 1989, Kuitca paints a blackened 12-part grid on a square canvas. In a Stations of the Cross-like progression, he portrays the house first in super-closeup, zeroing in on the bed, then pans to the dining room, then the bathroom, then gets further away and overhead now with the apartment floor-plan, then further away with a street plan, then a map of a city, then the state the city is in, and finally a white glowing shape in the same configuration as the apartment plan – perhaps the *soul* of the home; the abstracted *life force.* White ejaculatory stains dot some of the grid sections. Kuitca likes to telescope space. He likes to look at things from very close up and very far away. Additionally, he likes to show the sexual *charge* of the world.

Over and over he uses the apartment plan. Sometimes it cries clear bulbous teardrops (again a stigmata allusion), or padded like a madhouse cell (underscoring the prison aspect of the apartment), wet (as if sweating or alive), or circled in a crown of thorns (suffering and pain, as well as the mortification of the flesh), outlined in bones (death), sprouting arms and legs (anthropomorphizing horror, growth and a peculiar alien claustrophobia) and littered with syringes (the need to be anesthetized). In the 1990 *House Plan With Broken Heart,* Kuitca paints a Frida Kahlo-like red heart and other organs within this banished, otherwise empty place.

All the floor-plans are a remembering back – not Kuitca's remembering, but a collective remembering. Thus, they are commemorative or votive paintings meant as purgations, atonements or flagellations. Kuitca invents his own semi-Catholic iconography with the apartment a surrogate for the human body and the body of Christ. There is a *grand narrative* afoot in Kuitca's work. There's a powerful yearning to this phase of his work. It's not that Kuitca's religious – he's not – or that he's a proselytizer – he's not – but he's searching for clues to some vague mystery – looking for *reason* to believe.

These paintings aren't confessions. If they were they'd feel smaller (and more like the Story Art of the seventies) and less moving. They *bear witness* to the residual traces – the smoldering embers – of all our deepest recollections. These paintings are a collective memoir – vestiges of an emotional genesis from childhood to adulthood. They are like a labyrinth insofar as they are riddles without clues. But most of all they imply fantastic journeys or Joycean wanderings far afield.

As indicated, Kuitca likes to look at things from a distance so it should come as no surprise that maps make up the third rough category of his work. These are images of mostly unspecified places. (Anyone armed with an atlas could deduce what places these are, although in certain cases Kuitca 'doctors' the map, substituting names to suit his whimsy. So it's best not to place too great a significance on exactly where these places are. It's almost the equivalent of going in the wrong direction.) They link up with the all over abstract expressionist wing of painting, but also to a post-conceptual penchant for diagramming. Who doesn't like looking at maps? They're the wings we use to fly over places, the grid we superimpose on the natural and man-made world. We map what we need to know. With the maps, Kuitca takes on not only the forces at work on the self within the family, but now the forces at work on the family itself. With the maps, we also see Kuitca breaking out of his enclosed (cloistered), disenfranchised space and into the whole world and this increases the breadth of his work. Here he examines the secret lives of cities, the hidden dreams of countries and the day-to-day struggles of staying alive. The faceless power of nationhood now comes into focus.

Kuitca turns maps into complicated narratives – he de-neutralizes them. Looking at one of his maps is like having an exquisite flying dream – you're free of gravity and moving silently above it all, safe and tranquil – they're paintings with the sound track finally switched off.

Maps are fairly anonymous. They're mechanical projections of the world. Nevertheless, Kuitca's world view comes to bear in them as well. They're very hand-painted in spite of looking so perfect. Kuitca is on a pilgrimage to all over the world (this echoes the all over painting style he employs). He's definitely not local. There are maps of cities and countries and rivers from every corner of the globe: from Buenos Aires (home) to Minneapolis, from Scotland to Poland, from the Rhine to the Carpathians, and one is of the heavens.

Sometimes the streets are littered with syringes or painted red as if stained with blood. Other times, the same city name is repeated over and over suggesting the inescapable nature of certain places or maybe just the fact that the name has a melodic ring or a religious feel to it. Still other times he paints maps on beds in order to re-integrate the phantasmagoric role they always play in his work. The big, blowup scale of the maps is extremely satisfying too. Your eyes get lost in the veinal grid of roads and towns, street names and landmarks. They make for a lovely form of poetry. Place names, beautiful place names that mean so much with saying so little. The paintings are like lists this way, naming places and experiences, putting the world at your fingertips.

Once this guy left home, he just kept going. The maps have a heady lightness of being, an amplitude of spirit, and an infinite capacity for dreaming the world – and this separates them, somewhat, from the stage-sets and the floor-plans. It gives them a jaunty agile savoir-faire. Kuitca went looking for the world and he found it. This is the phase of his work that gives his whole project its final boost – makes it feel wide and solid. He could have stopped after the floor-plan paintings but he had so much more to say and was absolutely intent on finding ways to get it said. He's one of those artists who's not afraid to fail. He's always pushing his work, expanding its boundaries.

He has become so many characters. In addition to the aforementioned wayfarers, he's like Stephen Dedalus who wandered the streets of Dublin for twenty-four unforgettable hours in James Joyce's *Ulysses*. In fact, there's a terrific twenty-four-part gridded map of a place that might be Edinburgh which echoes Joyce's heroic journey. This untitled work from 1990 is like a black-and-white illuminated manuscript, or a slide show of some fantastic voyage one hour at a time. This gives the work a flat-footed importance, charges it with something epic. It traces footsteps of no one in particular bound for nowhere but nevertheless criss-crossing the streets of this city. Like a number of Kuitca's map paintings it also conjures up war maps or strategic planning diagrams: trial runs for bombing missions or other battle-plans. Because the maps are big and in God's eye-perspective they produce this omnipotence. His work takes us such vast distances so effortlessly that they acquire a science-fiction scale. They're like tales of worlds you and I will never see. This makes Kuitca seem so much more experienced than his years. This is what is meant when it is said 'his soul is old', that he has savoir-faire. Ultimately, Kuitca can feel like he's desperately trying to tell you of his travels across the emotional galaxy. Roy, the nexus-six replicant from the Ridley Scott film *Blade Runner,* comes to mind. Roy, who traveled all over the galaxy in search of a way to lengthen his six-year-programmed life span, finally gives up and says at the end of his life, 'You would not believe the things I've seen. I've seen attack ships on fire off the shores of Orion; C-beams glistening near the Tannhauser Gate. All these things will be lost in time...like tears in rain.' Kuitca evokes the fundamental sadness of life – namely that it ends – in these strange map paintings. You get the feeling that Kuitca's seen a lot of things and done a lot of living and you love him for this. He does things that for whatever reason you don't do. He does them for you. And this reminds you once again of the redemptive side of his work. There is an amazing grace to his work that makes your heart go out to him.

Most essays about Kuitca would end here. Or they might make one last plea for Kuitca as a 'political artist', claiming that his paintings are propaganda against fascism and oppression, and probably there is a grain of truth to this claim. But it's narrow and ultimately self-serving, and sells Kuitca short. He's not didactic. To say he is a failure to let the work open-up, and an attempt to colonize it in short-sighted ways. It's a way of not really seeing the paintings. So the story would end here by saying Kuitca's a good activist artist whose output stops with the maps, that he'll now rework these elements in new ways. Wrong! There is at least one more non-category that deserves mention and has never, to my knowledge, been dealt with before. I call that category (for want of a better name) The Songs and they reveal much about the artist's spirit, and they tell us that he's only picking up speed.

In at least ten cases (as far as I can determine) Kuitca has used either the titles of popular songs, or in several cases, painted the words of whole songs on scumbled or pictured backgrounds. The songs he has chosen are intriguing and they leave us a kind of treasure map to the inner recesses of Kuitca's soul. When you hear someone singing a song, in a way, you're getting across to some unconscious layer of the person and his or her thoughts. Singing de-activates defense mechanisms, it reduces inhibitions. Singing a song is like making a map – it's a way of making something your own. And this is obviously an important and recurring theme in Kuitca's work. We map what we need to know and we sing what we want to feel. Both are devices that provide access to our more secret sides, both are ways of getting things out without exposing them to too much danger. Mapping is fantasizing within a structure and so is singing the words to other people's songs. In some ways this is what looking at a painting is – a way to see what we didn't know we needed to see.

Kuitca has painted the words to The Beatles' *Strawberry Fields Forever* twice. In one of the two paintings he superimposes the words of the song over a scene of prisoners – presumably in a concentration camp (judging by the striped pajamas they're wearing, and how packed together they are) – happily mouthing the words of this song. The painting is a contradiction in terms. Obviously the song and the prisoners occupy two different times, not to mention two different emotional states of being. The words of the song are dreamy, innocent musings about faraway pretend places. Nothing could be more brutal than the world of the death camps. Kuitca's touch is so light here however that he gets this little image to pack quite a punch. You start thinking about what it takes to get through hard times, the depth of the human spirit and also the incredible lightness of it. It's an absurd image that comes in under your defenses and lodges in your psyche. The words of the song permutate into something dark and foreboding as when the phrase 'nothing to get hung about' resonates with awful implication. It's a corny image, to be sure, but it's also about escape, and a lot of Kuitca's work is about trying to get from here to *someplace else* (at least in the emotional sense).

He's painted a lyric from Simon & Garfunkel's *Bridge Over Troubled Water*. The lyric he chooses is about sacrifice. You always feel this strain of Kuitca wanting to lay his life down for another's. It's also an overly sentimental lyric and Kuitca likes to play with the over sentimental and the melodramatic. Songs allow him to step aside slightly and yet indulge in it. In another painting titled *Gimme Shelter* (after the Rolling Stones song of the same name) he's rendered the apartment plan in the words 'shelter me' – another allusion to isolation and the need for protection. A lot of the paintings seem to be about looking for love and connection.

In 1988 he painted *Porgy and Bess*. All the titles of the songs from Gershwin's musical *Porgy and Bess* are listed, as if on a record. Here Kuitca connects up with the artist Jean Michel-Basquiat whose penchant for incessant list making is well known. Kuitca's not as maniacal about it, but he's similarly predisposed to repetition and naming – of annexing other people's thoughts. (Perhaps it should be mentioned that he doesn't limit himself to songs in this regard. In 1988 he also painted a proto-floor-plan titled *The Potato Eaters* after an early work by Van Gogh.) So it becomes clearer that when Kuitca names something – whether it's a song or a city – he's making it his own.

But most telling may be the three canvasses that contain whole songs by Bruce Springsteen. There is a scene in the movie *Risky Business* in which the main character – a hormonal adolescent suburban boy – dressed only in his underwear begins undulating the minute his parents leave him home alone to a rock-'n-roll song blaring from the stereo. It's a great image. Something that feels familiar too. It's a form of masturbation and acting out. It's also a rebel yell, a cry for glory. A sexual plea. Songs are a way of saying what might otherwise be unsayable – maybe because they're so powerfully accurate. They're mantras of our imagination, maps of our secret desires. They are a way to *eavesdrop on the soul*. And the songs that Kuitca chooses here are really wails about 'breaking out' and 'getting free' and letting love 'blind us'.

These three songs (*Born to Run*, *Thunder Road* and *Cover Me*) show us a side that Kuitca usually keeps veiled. They're filled with pain and grandiose emotions in the face of overwhelming odds. They're songs about a yearning for a sense of power and physical experience. The people that Springsteen writes about (and therefore that Kuitca paints about), are pretty marginal characters – people on the edge of society, in danger of disappearing. People with little to lose and a lot to gain, bursting with a need to love or die or kill. They're amazingly romantic anthems for the lonely. They're sung to, about and by working-class heroes; guys (usually) stuck in dead-end jobs, living off the edge of where the action is, filled with self-loathing and unexpressed passions. The 'Songs' form the libretto to Kuitca's work. They are the way we know that he dreams, like we do, of 'letting go', of 'being safe', of 'getting away', of 'breaking through to the inside' – but most of all it puts us in close proximity to Kuitca's singularly 'human touch'.

Mi hijo es bello como el sol, 1982
Acrylic on wood
42 x 191 cm
Collection of the artist
Courtesy: Sperone Westwater, NY

Nadie olvida nada, 1982
Acrylic on wood
140 x 50 cm
Collection of the artist
Courtesy: Sperone Westwater, NY

Nadie olvida nada, 1982
Acrylic on wood
140 x 52 cm
Collection of the artist
Courtesy: Sperone Westwater, NY

El mar dulce, 1984
Acrylic on paper, mounted on canvas
200 x 400 cm
Collection: Sonia Becce, Buenos Aires

Tres días, 1986
Acrylic on canvas
213 x 235 cm
Collection: Marion and Jorge Helft,
Buenos Aires

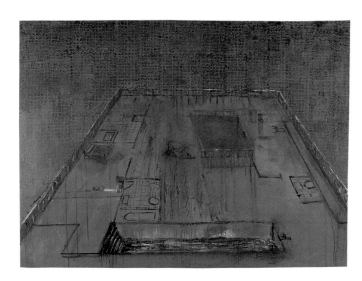

Untitled, 1988
Acrylic on canvas
150 x 200 cm
Collection: Marion and Jorge Helft,
Buenos Aires

Tres Noches, 1986
Acrylic on canvas
213 x 235 cm
Collection: Hugo Petruchanski, Buenos
Aires

148

House Plan with Teardrops, 1989
Acrylic on canvas
200 x 140 cm
Collection: Angela Gilchrist, NY
Courtesy: Annina Nosei Gallery, NY

Untitled, 1991
Acrylic on canvas
118 x 92 cm
Collection: Private, Geneva

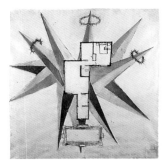

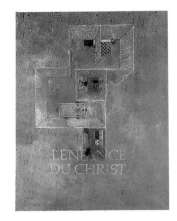

Holy Family, 1989
Acrylic on canvas
188 x 182 cm
Collection: Olle Johansson, Stockholm
Courtesy: Annina Nosei Gallery, NY

L'Enfance du Christ, 1989
Acrylic on canvas
198 x 147 cm
Collection: Seydoux, Paris
Courtesy: Annina Nosei Gallery, NY

Planta con texto, 1989
Acrylic and oil on canvas
200 x 140 cm
Collection of the artist
Courtesy: Sperone Westwater, NY

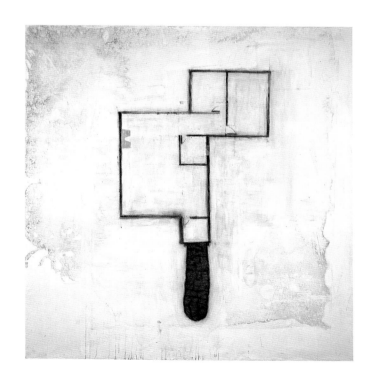

Shit Disposal House Plan, 1990
Acrylic on canvas
213 x 203 cm
Collection: Cesare Grazioli, Brescia
Courtesy: Gian Enzo Sperone, Rome

Esa persona en la que pienso, que es mi única esperanza después de todas las derrotas, está separada de mí por una pared y duerme. Pasado mañana montará a caballo. Lo llamarán rey. Ven hijito. Me duermo. Te llamarán con mi nombre. Voy a dormir. Quiero verte a caballo en sueños.

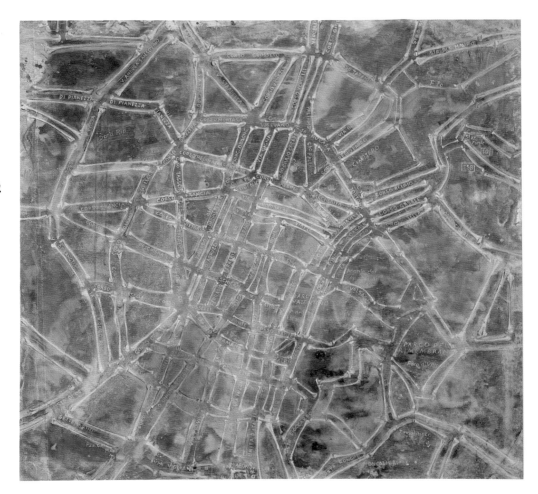

Torino, 1991
Acrylic on canvas
190 x 200 cm
Collection: Marco Brignone, Turin
Courtesy: Gian Enzo Sperone, Rome

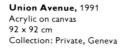

Union Avenue, 1991
Acrylic on canvas
92 × 92 cm
Collection: Private, Geneva

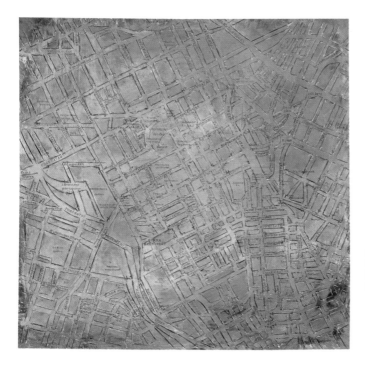

Cold Steel Streets, 1990
Acrylic on canvas
200 × 200 cm
Collection: Thomas Ammann, Zurich

Coming Home, 1989
Acrylic on canvas
137 x 137 cm
Collection: Teresa Serrano, NY
Courtesy: Anina Nosei Gallery, NY

Untitled, 1989
Offset
12 x 5.8 cm
Collection of the artist

Untitled, 1989
Offset
20.4 x 14.3 cm
Collection of the artist

Untitled, 1989
Offset
19.5 x 14 cm
Collection of the artist

Untitled, 1989
Offset
20.4 x 17.2 cm
Collection of the artist

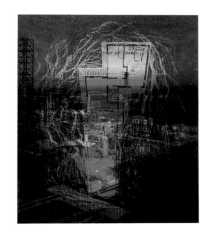

Children's Corner, 1990
Acrylic on canvas
140 x 140 cm
Collection: Museum Boymans van
Beuningen, Rotterdam
Courtesy: Galerie Barbara Farber,
Amsterdam

Todo el gas del mundo, 1989
Acrylic on canvas
176 x 329 cm
Collection: Massimo D'Alessandro,
Rome
Courtesy: Annina Nosei Gallery, NY

Oil Cross, 1988
Mixed media on canvas
140 x 140 cm
Collection: Julia Lublin, Buenos Aires
Courtesy: Galeria Julia Lublin, Buenos
Aires

Untitled, 1991
Mixed media on canvas
240 x 190 cm
Collection: Sperone Westwater, NY
Courtesy: Sperone Westwater, NY

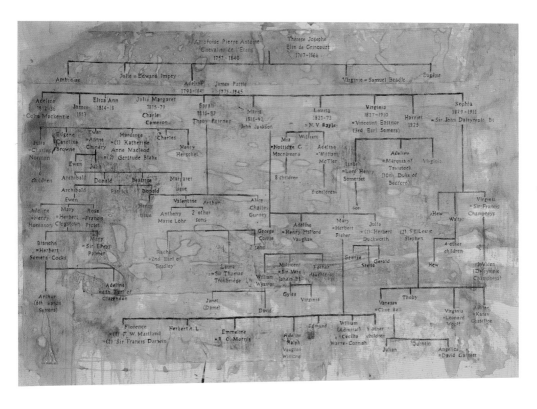

People on Fire, 1992
Acrylic on canvas
127 x 170 cm
Collection: Sperone Westwater, NY
Courtesy: Sperone Westwater, NY

The River, 1989
Mixed media on mattress
198 x 137 cm
Collection: Francesco Pellizi

Coming, 1988
Acrylic on canvas
140 x 100 cm
Collection: The Ranbir Singh Collection

Marcelo E. Pacheco

Guillermo Kuitca: A Painter's Inventory

Argentina: confines or possibilities?

Kuitca's paintings call for a particular viewer, someone who is prepared for a confrontation. Seeing is a dangerous game.

The intensity of historical developments in countries like Argentina implies a constant existential challenge, both on the social level and on that of the individual. Basic ingredients of this challenge are fear, the lack of social solidarity or even cohesion, the authoritarian power of the institutions, corruption, isolation, a perversion of the social, economic and political ties, the cohabitation of a legal order with another order that is fraudulent, a lack of historical consciousness, the liquidation of revolutionary, alternative or critical elements, an educational system whose content is worthless and an indifference to death.

Cultural constants like these form the reality and the context that Argentinean artists have to work with. The force of the message of the painters and sculptors of this region has to do with the fact that their context is a collective destiny that both contains and excludes permanently, that insists on commitment while punishing any decisive action, that both provokes and immobilizes but which at the same time is a familiar one, intimate in its reality.

The involvement of artists with this history gives them the function of active observers; they are witnesses. Their works are charged with the need to investigate reality, to exorcize destiny, their own and that of the collective, to imbue every form, color and material with an active, dynamic character.

Y la ciudad, ahora, es como un plano
De mis humillaciones y fracasos;
[...]
Aquí el incierto ayer y el hoy distinto
Me han deparado los comunes casos
De toda suerte humana;
[...]
Aquí mi sombra en la no menos vana
Sombra final se perderá, ligera.
No nos une el amor sino el espanto;
Será por eso que la quiero tanto.[1]

Argentina: a context in a mist

Between May and December 1982 Kuitca participated in four collective exhibitions in Buenos Aires: *Grupo IIIII* in the Centro de Arte y Comunicación (CAYC), *La Anavanguardia* in the

Untitled, 1991
Acrylic on canvas
74 x 92 cm
Collection: Gian Enzo Sperone, Rome
Courtesy: Gian Enzo Sperone, Rome

Si yo fuera el invierno mismo,
1986
Acrylic on canvas
137 x 190 cm
Collection: Marion and Jorge Helft,
Buenos Aires

Estudio Glesso, *La Nueva Imagen* and *Pintura Fresca,* both in the Galería del Buen Ayre. The choice of participants was both eclectic and heterogeneous; it included artists of different generations, working with different assumptions. Amongst them were Antonio Berni, Jorge de la Vega, Rómulo Macció, Diana Aisenberg, Luis Frangella, Armando Rearte, Duilio Pieri, Alfredo Prior, Marcia Schvartz, Pablo Suárez. The articles in the catalogues had a hard time trying to make sense of this bewildering mix of styles, images and concepts. Terms like neo-expressionism, Transavanguardia, New Image are used to explain these choices. They show how easily the concept of post-modernism with its conceptual baggage train can take up residence in the discourse of local criticism.

A terminology that belongs to other traditions – Germany, Italy and the United States – is unquestioningly imported to do the job of classifying the art of Argentina. One device is constantly employed: foreign stylistic categories are brought in with a view to organizing local history. The almost natural result is a profound estrangement between the discourse of theory – that acquires an almost exclusive autonomy – and the visual discourse that is forced to fit into alien and self-referring schemata. The phenomenon is both exceptional and endemic, now that language and image are beginning to travel along parallel paths. The conflict can be clearly seen if we try re-mixing the two discourses; visual works resist what is written about them and the spoken word does not have any basis either in the history of images or in cultural history. In this way the history of the region has constructed a hypothetical picture of the other history of art, concentrating on those areas that have escaped investigation: works, documentation, the realm of the plastic arts, the various currents of thought. Curiously enough this strategy was maintained and even validated in the eighties just when the definition of the post-modern condition provided theoretical justification for a divorce between the institutionalized model and the marginal variant. The eighties, of course, began with a polemic around post-modernism and with the search for a local generation that could be established as a correlative to the prevailing international trends. Neo-Expressionism in Germany and the Wild Painting movement; the Italian Transavanguardia; the new sculpture in Britain; post-modernism and the new painting in America; the new photo-graphy in Canada.

164

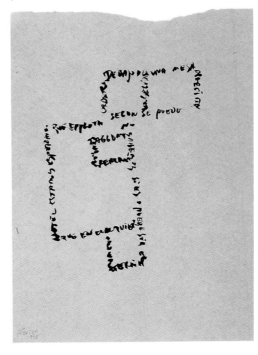

Untitled, 1990
India ink on canvas
28.3 x 19.8 cm
Collection of the artist

Carlos II a la guillotina, 1990
Watercolor and ink on paper
19 x 25.4 cm
Collection of the artist

Specific Pillow, 1990
Pencil and India ink on paper
19.1 x 26.2 cm
Collection of the artist

It is symptomatic that in Argentina post-modernism was planted on top of a modernism that, without anybody bothering to take a look at the patient, was pronounced as being in crisis. Inherent in the concept of post-modernism is that it has a definite place in chronology even though its implications are non-linear; it comes *after* the other term in the equation: modernism.

In the case of Latin America it is even difficult to know what modernism is. It is an alien process, introduced from abroad; the modern is a transplant here. The cultural horizon of Latin America is *different* and cannot be subjected to a concept that Europe uses to define itself. To do so is to build a hierarchy on the modernistic polarity between the center and the periphery. While a vague form of local modernism may be detected, one can hardly say with any confidence that this modernism has been in crisis nor that the crisis has led to the emergence of post-modernism. The latter movement also appears here as a transplant with origins in international fashion. In this way the general trend in Argentinean art history is reaffirmed, which aims to assimilate foreign discourses, while searching for a comprehensive key that would confer both value and meaning on local production.

It is obvious that artistic languages in the 20th century have been transformed into international codes that have a speedy almost instantaneous distribution and assimilation. The processes of the dissemination of images and theories accelerate the formation of stylistic trends and these spread world-wide propagating a homogeneity that, of course, also implies the imprint of heterogeneity between the centers that produce the models and the margins that adopt them.

What we are dealing with is a system of relations in which cultural geopolitics determines differences between a privileged circuit of innovation and another, peripheral, circuit that absorbs these innovations. In this way an otherness emerges that is rooted only in the degree of quality that separates the original artistic production from that 'other' production that is its reflection.

Adherence to the Western tradition becomes an automatic reflex by which manners, languages, discourses, images and theories that are alien to the particular character of local conditions are assimilated. The problem does not lie so much in the affirmation of an international cultural horizon nor in any participation in a process of 'globalization' – both of which are elements of an

Untitled, 1987
Acrylic on canvas
211 x 142 cm
Collection of the artist
Courtesy: Sperone Westwater,
New York

St. John Baptist, 1991
Ink on paper
19.9 x 28.4 cm
Collection of the artist

St. John Baptist, 1991
Acrylic on paper
19.9 x 28.3 cm
Collection of the artist

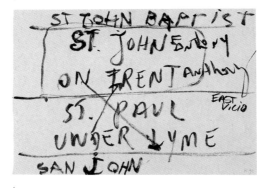

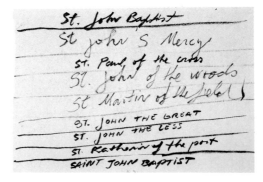

undeniable reality; rather it is caused by the compulsive and unthinking adoption of schemata that are not one's own.

It is curious to see that on the one hand the existence of political, social, economic and demographic categories indicating a profound difference between the developed and the underdeveloped countries, between a first world and a third, are acknowledged and that on the other hand when one comes to the realm of art these differences are treated as mere variants. Attention is focused on the difference between an original style and its provincial assimilation, as though that were the whole story. The horizon of the collective and the individual destiny is transformed into one more abstraction typical of the power play between North and South. The urgency of an everyday reality that would define histories and projects is neutralized and reduced to almost folkloristic local variations.

What kind of 'modernism' is it that is exhausted in Argentina? What kind of 'historicizing optimism' is falling prey to self-doubt? What one-way linear street of history has reached an abrupt end? What are these certainties that have been abandoned? What 'post-modernism' is being talked about, and when critics here say 'we' who are they referring to?[2] There are too many questions for us to be able so directly to embark on the eighties with post-modernism as our travelling companion.

In the same way as Pettoruti's Cubism and Xul Solar's Surrealism or the styles of Antonio Bernia and Jorge de la Vega are 'suspect', so are Kuitca's Transavanguardism, Neo-Expressionism and his New Image. Applied in this way, stylistic concepts no longer say anything; they become void and are converted into a means of assimilation by which works are enclosed within a relation of domination. The conceptual content disappears completely; all that remains are vague points of reference. The noun becomes an adjective.

'The perverse inflection that, due to the fragmented syntax of post-modernism, meant that it was the center that first began to meditate on the crisis in centralism and to vindicate the lateral proliferation of images, and has forced the Periphery [...] to draw its own axes of polemical confrontation once again.'[3]

Gimme Shelter, 1991
Ink on paper
34 x 22 cm
Collection of the artist

Bone Built for Eternity, 1991
Acrylic on canvas
140 x 200 cm
Collection: Caldic Collection,
Rotterdam
Courtesy: Galerie Barbara Farber,
Amsterdam

Bone Built for Eternity, 1990
Acrylic on canvas
160 x 140 cm
Collection: Gian Enzo Sperone, Rome
Courtesy: Gian Enzo Sperone, Rome

Kuitca in the context of Argentina

The members of the groups with whom Kuitca exhibited in 1982, the younger 'generation', were all painters born between 1947 and 1957. They therefore belonged to the generation just before Kuitca. For these artists the seventies had been a time of active involvement in the frenetic socio-political and cultural panorama of that decade that ended with military dictatorship, repression and economic chaos. With this event the utopian aspirations of that generation were brought to an abrupt close. Since the seventies the awareness of being a survivor has become a basic element in the reality of Argentina.

On the other hand the restoration of democracy in 1983 has always had the air of being the sequel to a prior project that failed and which, as though it were a natural occurrence, left an empty space for the transition from a military regime to constitutional government. After la Guerra de las Malvinas (the Falklands War) of 1982 the fate of the dictatorship was sealed; a return to democracy was the only way out of what was effectively an impasse. The military junta had proved incapable of uniting the population. Even though Kuitca had his first one-man show in 1974 and though his works during those years displayed a direct relation with a vital local reality, the Falklands War was the first historical event to give him the sense of a common destiny that was specifically Argentinean.

'At the time of la Guerra de las Malvinas I started painting little beds... at that time I was going through a depression; what I wanted to convey in my work was that my hand and brush did not move at all; the painting was the result of the canvas moving. What it painted was hardly a sketch. My hand was not strong enough to grasp the brush firmly.'[4]

Kuitca appeared on the scene alongside those artists in Buenos Aires who were creating an imagery and strategy that was typical of the early eighties. They were the heirs of the various stylistic and theoretical trends of the seventies, years which could now be seen as being imprisoned between the limits imposed on them by the explosion of the sixties and the new initiatives of the young groups emerging in the eighties. The only activity that did not fit into these confines was that of the CAYC group that was influenced by conceptual art and the art of systems. The work of this group, however, often feels like a one-way street.

Untitled, 1981
Mixed media on paper
21.7 x 27.8 cm
Collection of the artist

Untitled, 1992
Pencil on paper
7 x 49 cm
Collection of the artist

Buenos Aires, febrero 23 de 1982.-

Señor Director
del Museo de Arte

Untitled, 1982
Ink on paper
33.5 x 21.7 cm
Collection of the artist

K 81

VOY A TOMARME TRES ROHIPNOL, EL PRIMERO PARA DROGARME, EL SEGUNDO PARA DORMIRME Y EL TERCERO PARA SOÑAR

In Argentinean art history, historical discourses – unlike historical events – seem to come in waves of strong and weak decades; moments of great intensity continue to have an impact on years that are more 'lukewarm' and are less influential. For instance, the eruption of a modernism that was developed and sustained by artists, critics and writers in the decade of the twenties was followed by the more neutral activity of the Grupo de Paris in Buenos Aires in the thirties. The innovations of the forties were the result of the dynamic activity of groups that were involved with concrete art; the fifties were an almost natural prolongation of them. The informalism of that decade was basically a reaction of lyrical abstraction against the rationally and geometrically-based, non-figurative forms of the Asociación Arte Concreto-Invención, of the Madí and the 'Perceptismo' groups. Typical of the sixties was their urgent need to communicate and their great creative originality – the decade was dominated by the Instituto Di Tella and its associates; they were followed by the more complex and less sharply defined decade of the seventies.

The younger generation that became active in 1982 – a date that has become an artificial landmark – grew up in a climate where conceptual art prevailed. Once again there was a reaction. A group of painters emerged who defended painting as a basic medium, and who saw visual perception as the viewer's essential activity. In the previous decade painting had often been declared dead; this attitude was replaced by a new burst of painterly activity. This did not just mean that painting as a language was once more acknowledged; every aspect of the profession was paid homage. This was achieved by a use of colors and textures to create a powerful imagery, by the size of the canvases and by the physical tactility of these paintings. In short, figuration was once again 'in'.

It is true that, connected with or parallel to the activity of the conceptual artists, there were also painters and sculptors in the seventies – Berni, Alonso, Pablo Suárez and Heredia, for instance – who had continued the tradition of painting as a medium and of figurative work, while allowing the presence of concepts to determine the visual codes they adopted. In the same way the painting of ideas continued to be an essential ingredient for the generation of the eighties; we only need to glance at the work of Kuitca and other painters of this decade to see this.

Untitled, 1981
Pencil and ink on paper
35 x 50 cm
Collection of the artist

Untitled, 1981
Charcoal, pencil and India ink on paper
17.5 x 25 cm
Collection of the artist

Untitled, 1981
Mixed media on paper
30 x 34.5 cm
Collection of the artist

1NO

2OS

3RES

4UATRO

5INCO

6EIS

7IETE

8CHO 1NO

Untitled, 1981
Acrylic on paper
25 x 17.5 cm
Collection of the artist

The common element in their work is their ideological attitude. These painters began their careers when conceptual art was the dominant movement; their response was to make a cause of the rescue of painting as material, as profession and as language. The result was painting but by painters whose approach was conceptual. There are other elements that they had in common: their imagery, for instance, and the stylistic codes they employed; they developed, however, independently of each other. Unreal figures, large theatrical spaces, self-referring fictions and the equivocal atmosphere of their paintings; Kuitca's iconography uses the same references; their semantic content, however, is different. Enigmatic elements, a use of segmentation, humour, ambiguity, sensuality; an emotional intensity and a defiance of established limits – these are the elements they had in common.

The generation gap, however, placed Kuitca in a quite exceptional historical position. The ties resulting from exhibitions and groups at the beginning of the eighties rapidly dissolved because they had been formed under the pressure of a prior theoretical discourse and were not the product of any genuine meeting of minds. After 1985, moreover, Kuitca's work was regularly exhibited in Europe. He acquired an international reputation that was sealed by his one-man show in the 'Projects' series in the Museum of Modern Art (MoMA) and by his presence at the 9th Documenta in Kassel in 1992. This meant that just at the point when his generation – 1957/1963 – was making a name for itself in Buenos Aires – the Grupo de la X, founded in 1987 but discontinued; the influential group of artists around the Centro Cultural Ricard Rojas el Rojas; the provocations of Miguel Harte and Marcelo Pombo; independent activity by artists such as Reyna, Eduardo Alverez, Daniel Garcia, Siquier and Garófalo[5] – Kuitca was carving out a space for himself, first of all in Europe and then in the United States.

This meant that Kuitca's career developed in isolation from developments in Buenos Aires; he remained marginal both to the previous generation, which he belonged to 'artificially', and to his own generation because of this early lacuna in his professional career. In the end this peculiar situation would only have been a footnote in Argentinean art history if it weren't for the 'Kuitca syndrome' that has emerged in Buenos Aires today.

In Argentinean art history there is no precedent

Untitled, 1983
Ink on paper
20.7 x 28.8 cm
Collection of the artist

Untitled, 1983
India ink on paper
29 x 27.7 cm
Collection of the artist

Untitled, 1983
India ink on paper
28 x 25 cm
Collection of the artist

Untitled, 1983
India ink on paper
28 x 25 cm
Collection of the artist

for the phenomenon of Kuitca's international reputation that developed so suddenly and with such vitality[6], coinciding as it did with a distinct decline of his impact on the local scene. His last one-man show in Buenos Aires, for instance, was in 1986. To the degree that Kuitca established his reputation as an Argentinean artist abroad, however, his influence in his own country has become an echo of his achievements abroad. His work is *appropriated,* but is not exhibited and it has become indistinct in direct proportion to the expansion of his image as a successful artist.

A curious phenomenon occurs then of the separation of the painter from his production. Today Kuitca is known for the list of his exhibitions in Europe and the USA, for the soaring prices paid for his paintings in New York art sales and for the reputation of the foreign art critics who wrote the introductions for his catalogues.

Where then does this place his paintings? How can one define the mature work of this artist who, when he suddenly emerged in the public domain in the eighties, was celebrated as one of the discoveries of that moment?

The show begins

Coming is a suggestive word for a title of a painting. In isolation and lacking in any grammatical context, it gets its impact from its sound and atmosphere.

The word 'coming' has a hidden meaning. The imagery, suggestive as the title but less mysterious, shows us a world and constructs a meaning. A network of horizontal and vertical lines and twelve fields to discover, twelve possibilities to explore. A web composed of things that have been lost and of the memory of a painter in Buenos Aires. In 1989 Guillermo Kuitca painted his second version of *Coming*. It is a work that serves as an emblem or as an imaginary thread through his own labyrinth. A bed, an empty room, a bath, the map of a neighbourhood, the name of a city, the ground plan for a house; a spotlight, light bulbs that shine for nobody, words that function as decoys, houses, streets and roads; a sense of something moist and throbbing, traces of sperm.

Since the series he painted in 1982, *Nadie olvida nada o Antiedipo,* beds have become a key motif, a constant of his painterly and semantic flow of ideas. This everyday item of furniture, that has such an elemental relation with birth, sickness,

Untitled, 1982
India ink on paper
19 x 26 cm
Collection of the artist

176

Untitled, 1985
Color pencil on paper
21 x 27 cm
Collection of the artist

Untitled, 1989
Pencil on canvas
27.5 x 22 cm
Collection of the artist

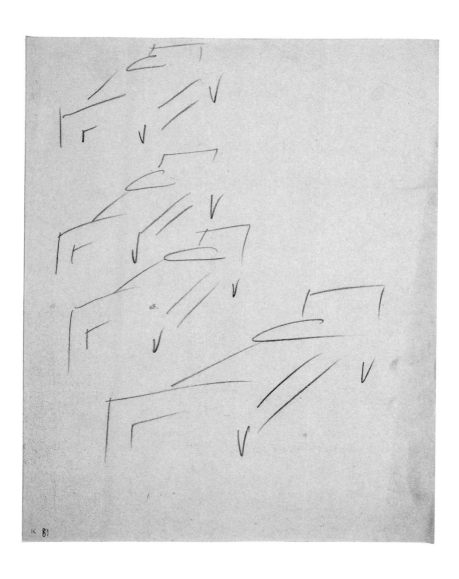

dreams and death, is an ever-recurring presence. The bed is almost always empty. It stands there in the intimacy of a deserted room or else it floats in a space that is painted a crude yellow or else it resembles a property in some theatrical set. When it is occupied, the place of repose becomes a domain of fear in the nightmare of a helpless child, threatened with death by his mother. It is also the solitude of tears and separation; it is a bed in flames or submerged in water; it is an anonymous bed repeated obsessively in its isolation and emptiness. But a bed is also a synonym for sexual passion; it is transgression and taboo, possession and subversion. It is the place of eroticism: the ineluctable presence of violence. The movement is vertiginous and climactic, its depiction is intense but at the same time cautious and meticulously treated. These beds, whether occupied or empty, small or exaggeratedly large, are a constant presence; they stand for the possibility of desire, yet they also represent the abyss, they arouse fear, they are connected with our childhood nightmares, with the definition of sexuality as pain, with punishments for transgression inflicted on us by both family and society, with forbidden joys. These beds are the *mise en scène* for a tenderness that is postponed or a fulfilled desire. In *Coming* one of the beds even contains the signs of sexual encounter with its splashes of sperm. At the other corner of the painting, another bed is lit by a spotlight. The white light emphasizes its fictional character, the sense of absence: It is an *empty* bed. And next to it is a chair, the other everyday object that is a leitmotif in the painter's iconography.

In the series *El mar dulce* (1983-87), *Idea de una pasión* (1985), *Yo como...* (1985), *Siete últimas canciones* (1986), *Si yo fuera el invierno mismo* (1986) and, after 1987, his ground plans for houses and street plans of cities, chairs recur constantly. Once again Kuitca confronts us with an everyday object that, by being constantly repeated and because of its emptiness, becomes a metaphor for loneliness. He treats these everyday objects with great violence; they are almost invisible in their anonymity but, despite their isolation, they are protagonists. The artist's ego imposes itself on them giving them a new and disturbing vitality.

The chairs also look chaotic, they have fallen over or are broken. They are vestigial witnesses of an activity whose nature the viewer can only guess at. The empty chairs remind us that someone was there who has gone away. They are situated in

178

Siete últimas canciones, 1986
Acrylic on canvas
140 x 170 cm
Collection: Private, Buenos Aires

Untitled, 1984
Charcoal on paper
12 x 20 cm
Collection of the artist

El mar dulce, 1985
Oil on canvas
150 x 200 cm
Collection: Private, Brussels

huge spaces in which the presence of human beings is either minimized or entirely eliminated: human figures are reflected in mirrors or else they are phantasmagoric silhouettes from a dream state or from late-night wakefulness. The character of these objects as protagonists converts these scenarios into spaces without any narrative. There is no history here in a chronological sense. Time is condensed in the motionless image of a bed or a chair. This unreal atmosphere is emphasized by the spotlights; Kuitca's stage designs also include tape-recorders, microphones, curtains and tables, that serve to confirm the absence of any real personas. Loss and abandonment is what we see; this is human existence in its essential isolation and disintegration. The chair that is such a familiar object, that symbolizes meetings and encounters, that is a metaphor of human beings as social and communal animals, becomes another empty site. The appearance of the spotlight above the bed in *Coming* also refers to the body of the painter's work from 1983 to 1987. These are the years in which he defined the painted space essentially as a theatrical scenario with a characteristic ambiguity: the figures betray a learnt code; their movements are frozen into theatrical gestures within spaces that have the look of stage sets specially constructed for this action or which reveal familiar rooms peopled by an everyday normality. Kuitca was in fact active for a time as director of his own theatre company. In 1982 he directed his first production *Nadie olvida nada,* in partnership with Carlos Ianni and in 1984 he produced the work *El mar dulce* whose subject is the waves of immigrants who sail up the Rio de la Plata to Argentina. Both productions were put on in the Teatro Planeta in Buenos Aires. The two pieces were accompanied by two corresponding series of paintings, with the same name and painted at the same time.

The theatricality of Kuitca's canvases is also connected with the performances of Pina Bausch's Wuppertal Dance Theatre in 1980 in Buenos Aires that had a great influence on him. Pina Bausch's choreographies and sets are a challenge to the spectator who is overwhelmed by the frenetic movement, the obsessive repetition, the sequences of grotesque and terrifying images, the disturbing and suspect quality of her cryptic personas.

The work of the Wuppertal Dance Theatre is based on improvisations that are worked on during rehearsals and on the personal experience

180

Si yo fuera el invierno mismo,
1986
Acrylic on canvas
140 x 252 cm
Collection: Javier Benitez, Monterrey

Untitled, 1981
Charcoal on paper
34.5 x 25.5 cm
Collection of the artist

Untitled, 1985
Charcoal on paper
26 x 20 cm
Collection of the artist

Untitled, 1986
India ink on gray paper
22 x 23 cm
Collection of the artist

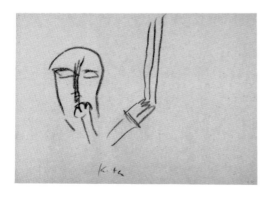

Untitled, 1984
Charcoal on paper
18.8 x 25.8 cm
Collection of the artist

of the individual dancers; these devices from her working methods are put on stage for the spectator to see. In the same way the actual reality of Kuitca's profession as painter is included in the surface of each of his canvases. This explains the immediacy of his imagery. 'What I show here are Pina Bausch's themes: relations between human beings and the lies that exist within these relations; the dread of loneliness, but above all the fear of everything that might interrupt this loneliness. Fugitives behind fortifications that guarantee survival, they search for a truth that is denied by conventional wisdom. All of this is emphasized with an insistent wit, that is sometimes on the verge of a kind of mania. But the despair about our human condition is helpless rather than cynical.'[7]

It was the intensity and provocative character of Pina Bausch's themes that had such a powerful influence on the painter. The Wuppertal Dance Theatre was also the revelation of a visual code; it validated the strategy he used for constructing imagery and deploying his symbolic world. In Pina Bausch's work there is a method of 'narrative' in which theatre, dance, music and film intersect as an essential underpinning for the scenic spectacle. Between these different languages there are no borders, only points of convergence. And Kuitca's painting is also just that, a tissue in which various codes intersect: theatre, film, literature, music. Painting is his chosen mode; but with him painting is only an instrument of expression that combines all the other possibilities. His visual language refers constantly to other sources, both formally and in a conceptual sense.

Around 1989 the range of his extra-pictorial borrowings became particularly rich. With the series of maps and house plans, his visual exploration has begun to refer to itself, rather than looking for additional elements from outside. This process is linked to the gradual stripping away of iconographical elements that is also a typical feature of Kuitca's painting. A greater austerity begins to appear. There is a definite direction and a more intense and concentrated exploration. This tendency has been evident since 1989, the year when he produced *Coming,* a painting that functions as a transitional point in his work. It is the return and the zero point that can be seen in eleven of the twelve compartments in this work. The number twelve is the seed, the origin; it is the ejaculation the painter needs in order to begin his game all over again.

Untitled, 1992
Mixed media on canvas
155 x 155 cm
Collection: Sperone Westwater,
New York
Courtesy: Sperone Westwater,
New York

Idea de una pasión, 1984
Acrylic on canvas
120 x 150 cm
Collection: Private, Buenos Aires

Untitled, 1992
Mixed media on canvas
195 x 218.7 cm
Collection: Sperone Westwater,
New York
Courtesy: Sperone Westwater,
New York

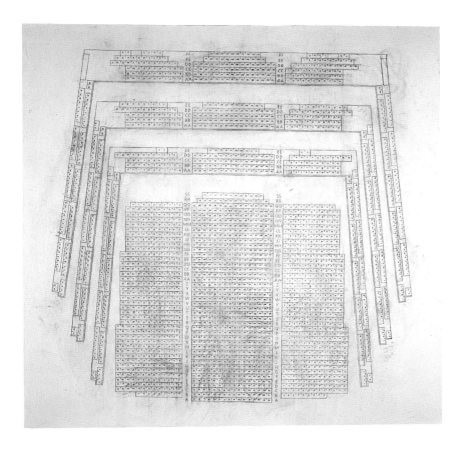

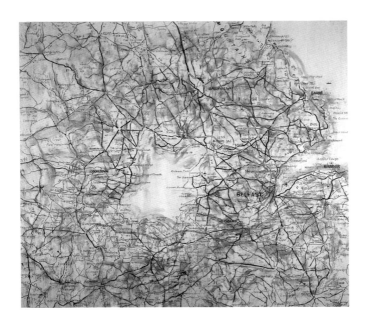

Kuitca in search of a house

So far, then, we have looked at two leitmotifs – the bed and the chair – and a method – theatricality – that are basic features of his work between 1982 and 1987 and are clearly referred to in *Coming*. The first version of the painting also shows two other rooms of the artist's 'house': the dining room and the bathroom. The two images get their force from their mutual opposition. The dining room, normally the place where the family comes together – is empty; it is tenanted only by furniture and a lighted light bulb. It is anonymous and impersonal. Nothing is happening here; nor are there any memories. The vitality of this space is annihilated by being stripped down to a grey existence. The bathroom, on the other hand, is a place full of anxiety; it is transformed by the ejaculation. Obvious traces of semen 'fertilize' this image. Perhaps an episode in a love story was enacted there – or was it just someone masturbating? One feels the vibrations of a sensuality that has passed and gone. For the spectator it represents a new anxiety.

We have now looked at the main rooms of the house with their ambiguities and their absent presences – plus the suggestive cadence of the title that is included in the painting. In two other compartments of *Coming* we see two general views of the house: an axonometric projection and a ground plan.

Since 1987 Kuitca has drawn on these two typical techniques of architectural design – it is yet another borrowing, another model from outside painting that he includes in his work. The experience of everyday space begins to recede and to come under control. We are no longer dealing with a depiction of familiar normal and everyday places; instead he employs an artificial language with its own rules of interpretation, with the code used by architects. We are no longer faced with the reality we live in, but with the schematization of that reality. The painter takes his distance and tries to treat his *mise en scène* with objectivity. Architecture was always an element in his works, but up until now it appeared in the form of rooms where walls, columns, staircases and windows were made of painted cardboard; they were stage curtains. His interiors were characterized by the presence of the transitory, by a sense of huge spaces. Since 1987, however, when his house plans and architectural projections first appear, the space is no longer an a priori space but a constructed one.

Untitled, 1991
Acrylic on canvas
110 x 60 cm
Collection: N.V. Bouwfonds
Nederlandse Gemeenten
Courtesy: Galerie Barbara Farber,
Amsterdam

Gran corona de espinas, 1989
Acrylic on canvas
200 x 300 cm
Courtesy: Galerie Barbara Farber,
Amsterdam

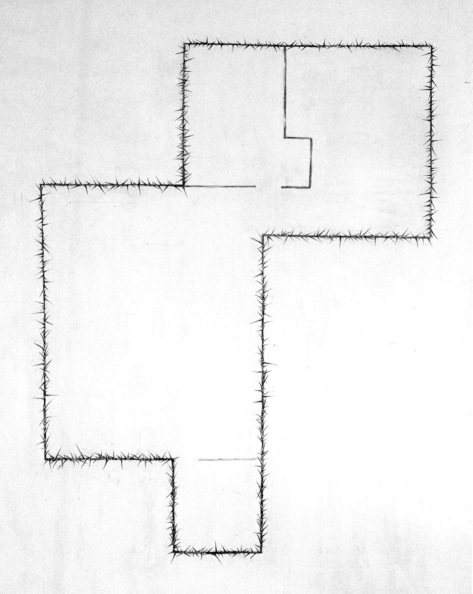

Order is established and our real experience of space is reduced to mathematics. The visual, tactile and psychological space of his earlier work is replaced by one that is metrical, objective and rational. Fragmentation, extension and multidirectionality are replaced by abstraction on the figurative level. 'The homogeneity of the geometrical space is ultimately based on a situation in which all its elements, the points it contains, are simply indicators of position, where they only refer to each other, no longer possessing any particular or autonomous content.'[8]

186

Kuitca proceeds to reformulate his ground plans and architectural projections by adding to the 'points' that define the structure other elements that are indicative of 'position': in other words, his beds and chairs reappear.

In 1987 the main theme of his imagery is an encounter between a cast of objects and abstract designs on the one hand – the architectural views, the obsessive characters of his iconography, the daily objects and nocturnal figures – and the sensory character of the materials of painting on the other – smudges, drips and textures. There is no loss of drama; rather the drama acquires greater concentration. After five years of work in which his narrative discourse was based on a collection of symbols and on complex encounters that take place in huge spaces, the painter has now reached a moment of synthesis. Here there are no declamations or sweeping theatrical gestures, but a new severity. The viewer is confronted now with a symbolic austerity whose effect is immediate. It is a moment of exploration. This new economy of means – simpler but not more rudimentary – is due to the ground plans that always seem to belong to the same house that has established itself as a prototype with its dining-room, kitchen, bathroom and two other rooms. In some versions of the house plans a figure of a child kneeling on the ground also appears; this is a presence that Kuitca has included in his paintings since the time of *Nadie olvida nada*.

The child plays different roles in different paintings. These roles have a common denominator, however: isolation and sorrow. Alone and punished by being stood in a corner of the room *(Nadie olvida nada, 1982)*; crawling on all fours with shoes on his hands *(Idea de una pasión, 1984)*[9]; sobbing on a table *(Vaga idea de una pasión, 1985)*; the motionless witness of the deeds of adults that he does not understand *(Si yo fuera el invierno mismo, 1986)*; naked with his

Nadie olvida nada, 1982
Acrylic on masonite
122 x 154 cm
Collection of the artist
Courtesy: Sperone Westwater,
New York

Vaga idea de una pasión, 1984
Acrylic on canvas
140 x 160 cm
Collection: Mary and Jaime Kuitca,
Buenos Aires

genitals pressed against a column *(El mar dulce,* 1986); looking at himself in the water and reliving the myth of Narcissus *(Siete úlimas canciones,* 1986); or as sole inhabitant of an empty house that is painted a ferocious red color *(Sin título,* 1988). In all these paintings we are confronted with sorrowful journeys to the lost world of infancy; visions of a non-existent tenderness, of an extreme loneliness and a primal terror.

Kuitca paints with words

At the same time as he was producing his first architectural projections and ground plans of houses, Kuitca also produced a series of self-referring acrylic paintings: they are the 'painted words'. This is a collection of canvases with a vertical format – in contrast with the normal horizontal layout – with a theme of night landscapes of factories, stations and city scenes, accompanied, or rather validated by literary texts that are superimposed on the painted imagery. The inclusion of written signs in his paintings is a constant of his creative method. The inclusion of the title in the work itself is a common element in the sketches he made in 1980 or in works like the two versions of *Tres noches* in 1985 and 1986 and *El mar dulce* in 1987. The presence of his own monogram *K,* that completely papers over the high walls of his interiors, occurs regularly in some oil paintings of 1985. Titles like these will continue to be a frequent device over the next few years; for instance, *El momento más hermoso de la guerra* (1987), *Asma* (1988), *Bridge Over Troubled Water* (1987-88) and, of course, the two versions of *Coming* from 1988 and the 'emblematic' version of 1989.
These canvases from 1987, however, form a whole that has a value in itself. The presence of texts, from a number of different sources, suggests that there is a direct link between the words and the images. The sentences are illustrated with specific images that serve as clues to their interpretation. The words are not a key to the meaning of the paintings, as in the case of the titles that he includes in other paintings; what we have here is a written and illustrated code, a round trip between the literary space and the painted one. The word does not designate a plastic world; rather it names an image, validating it for the viewer. 'I will sleep when I am dead', 'Before the familiar images I wondered...', 'Let me take you down...', 'When a dream dies, a lot of blood will flow' – these are some of the texts. In

188

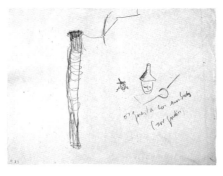

Untitled, 1983
Pencil on paper
21.5 x 27.8 cm
Collection of the artist

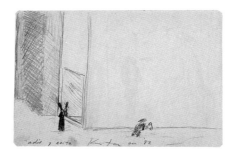

Adan y Evita, 1982
Pencil on paper
24 x 35 cm
Collection of the artist

Judith y Holofernes, 1982
Pencil on paper
23.8 x 34.8 cm
Collection of the artist

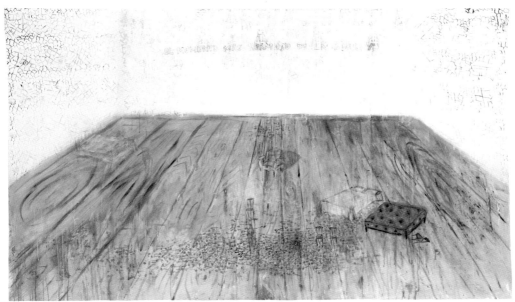

**El momento mas hermoso de la
guerra,** 1987
Acrylic on canvas
140 x 233 cm
Collection: Galerie Barbara Farber,
Amsterdam
Courtesy: Galerie Barbara Farber,
Amsterdam

Tres noches, 1986
Acrylic on canvas
140 x 180 cm
Collection: Private, São Paulo

each case there is a poetic link with the images.
As we have seen, this cluster of works dates from
1987 which was a pivotal year for Kuitca; it was in
this year that he began his process of stripping
away his iconography and making the
concentrated use of symbols mentioned above.
This was also the origin of the zero point in
Coming.
During this period of stylistic concentration, the
'painted words' series was merely a direction that
was explored only to be abandoned; there is
however an intimate relation between it and the
literary atmosphere of the greater part of his early
production. The painter is pivoting around
himself; he abandons structural motifs, such as the
chairs and the beds and the lonely child, as well as
his *mises en scène* and his whole theatrical manner,
as though it were unnecessary baggage. The house
plans and painted words explore new possibilities
of painting and of meaning. Between 1988 and
1989 Kuitca will embark on a new relation with
his profession, a different imagery and another
channel of communication with the viewer.

Kuitca becomes a tourist

In this process *Coming* is clearly a landmark; it was
my point of departure, the one I treat as an
'emblematic' work. We saw that six of the
compartments of this painting are allocated to
rooms and to views of a house. The five remaining
compartments refer us to another typical feature
of Kuitca's work, his street plans and maps of
regions. In this particular instance it is a
neighborhood in Hamburg and a section of the
surrounding region. Each compartment serves as a
play of distancing in five movements: an
assemblage of buildings with schematized facades;
their siting in a more general view of the
neighborhood; a detailed street plan, without
however the presence of recognizable elements
such as blocks of houses but where the name of
Hamburg is painted; a complex drawing of the
approach roads to the city; and finally the map of
the region where Hamburg is marked by a flashing
light.
This process of distancing occurs in stages and the
same is true of the objectifying of the
representational code. The traces that might
identify the facades dematerialize in the
impersonal character of an aerial view; they
dissolve into a cartography, the conventional
method for representing the spaces that surround
us.

190

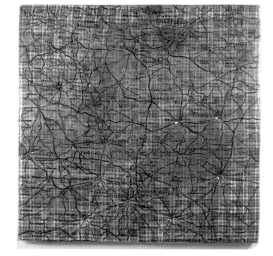

Untitled, 1992
Mixed media on mattress
200 x 200 cm
Collection: Gian Enzo Sperone, Rome
Courtesy: Sperone Westwater,
New York

Plano de Madrid, 1987
Acrylic on canvas
143.5 x 138 cm
Collection: Marion and Jorge Helft,
Buenos Aires

His first city maps, *Hamburg, Prague, Madrid* and *Buenos Aires sobre 'Mullah'*, as well as regional maps like Odessa, date from 1987; they take their place alongside the investigations of the views of houses and the 'painted words'. The image of a map is an artificial construct expressing cultural identity. They are an affirmation of our dominion over nature. They chart our existence on the surface of an agreed convention.

The contradiction in Kuitca's maps is that they undermine their basic function of orientation: This scheme of roads and signs for urban arteries is a new, invented geography; it is an act of painting, the product of a convention that has been subverted. Just as his architectural perspectives lose their functional homogeneity and are transformed into spaces of visual and symbolic narrative, so his views of cities and regions are full of visual and semantic hints. The painter turns a name such as Hamburg into a place that stands for a history; cartography becomes an imaginative space. These are maps seen by a painter who appropriates the pictorial character of these surfaces composed of lines, points, color and visual signs. There is an obvious play between the figurative character of the maps and street plans and the abstract purpose that transforms them into an artistic motif. Like the house plans, his topography is an appropriation; it incorporates a language that is much more strictly defined and whose rules are fixed in advance.

Kuitca's decision of 1987 to use prestructured conventions as his point of departure gave him the space to develop new ideas. By adapting his working method to professional and generally accepted models, such as those of architectural design and topography – he succeeded in creating new means of expression. The technique of appropriating preexistent material had a liberating function. The oppressive expansiveness of his previous imagery now becomes more peaceful. Some of his obsessions have been transcended. Instead a definite confrontation between imagery and craftsmanship begins to develop.

His first style of painting covered five years of unceasing productivity. Its elements included: large virtual spaces; an obvious and casual craftsmanship; a literary narrative; appropriations from literature, music and films as a constant element in his store of imagery; repeated depictions of various situations and occurrences where human beings are absent, at least in an affective sense, the encounters that there are between his characters always being compulsive

192

House with AIDS, 1987
Acrylic on canvas
157 x 214 cm
Collection: Marion and Jorge Helft, Buenos Aires

Vienna, 1990
Acrylic on canvas
213 x 187 cm
Courtesy: Annina Nosei Gallery, New York

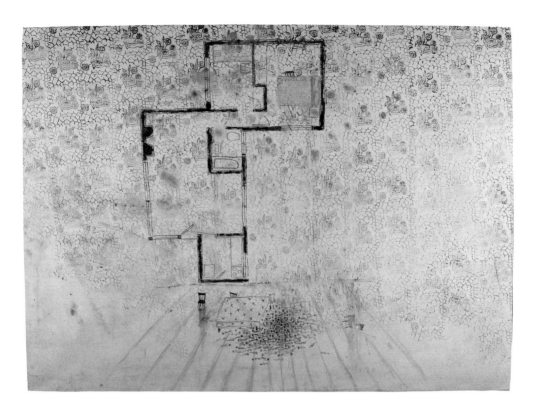

Untitled, 1990
Acrylic on canvas
11 parts, 20 x 30 cm each part
Collection: Private, Amsterdam
Courtesy: Galerie Barbara Farber,
Amsterdam

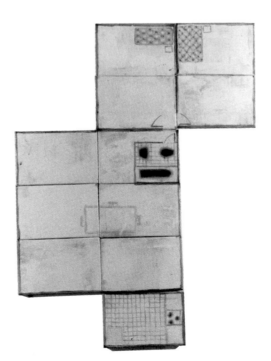

and violent. The figures in these paintings do not have any real existence, they have no body or weight; the real protagonists here are things. Theatricality is not a style applied from outside; rather it is the essential ingredient of his language: theatrical actions and rooms that clamour for everyday life.

The artist conceals in order to reveal

Since this crucial year of 1987, Kuitca has begun to explore possibilities, such as street plans of cities, maps, paintings with painted texts.

Essential works such as *House with AIDS* (1987), *Buenos Aires sobre 'Mullah' de Gibert & George* (1987), *Strawberry Fields Forever* (1988), *Porgy and Bess* (1988), *Futura* (1988) and *Coming* (1988), represent a move away from his previous style and suggest new directions and possibilities. A greater concentration emerges with specific images painted on a reiterated background of ground plans, maps, grids, panoramas. The pictorial play is enriched here almost to the point of exploding; its astonishingly sensory character is sustained by a profound understanding of color and craftsmanship. At the same time the iconography contracts, and is reduced to the painter's basic obsessions: beds, chairs, lonely children, words. Fear, desire, punishment, death and an atmosphere of menace remain; they are expressed, however, in more elementary imagery. This trend culminates in 1989, when he produced his first maps on mattresses. Painting breaks with its traditional ground. Pictures are transformed into three-dimensional objects.

One step further and the traditional spacial organization is also altered: His imagery is now presented on real beds that are arranged in space. With a single gesture the painter appropriates the material world, breaking with the painted metaphor and using beds as his true mode of expression. By hanging matresses or arranging beds in space, Kuitca creates a violent tension between the art object and the viewer.

In this context *Coming* is the painting that synthesizes the whole development. Its different compartments contain his previous themes and original obsessions, together with interiors and his more recent appropriation of axonometric projections and facades. But new possibilities can also be seen here, ones that, after careful consideration, will take over his work: his house plans and his maps. From now on these will serve as formal backgrounds for the works that he

Preparation for the Valencia project, 1992

produced in 1990 and 1991. But these two basic elements have been purified and refined since they first appeared in his paintings in 1987.

The house plans have now become a shape in themselves, as we have already seen in *Coming*. They work now as a parent structure with a plastic value and are no longer defined in relation to other forms. His street plans and maps of regions also increasingly appear as objects; the cities disappear as organizing centers or else they are obsessively repeated, so that they cease to be points of reference on the map.

In both these formal models the process is clear: a subtle balance between geometrical abstraction and vital expression; between formal rigour and the sensory deployment of materials and color. Both the outlines of the houses and the streets that make up the ground plan of the city, are converted into visual metaphors; their objective character – that existed prior to ground plan or street plan – is metamorphosed into thorns, syringes, swords and bones. Death, pain and punishment continue to be present, but now a single element is enough to convey this sense of despair. Kuitca has succeeded in creating a total unity between the plastic form and the message it contains; there is no allegory or elucidation. The image strikes home immediately as if it is grabbing one by the throat.

The character of the materials completes this visual play. Kuitca's technical skill is astonishing; more important, however, is the maturity he displays here as an artist. He almost seems to concentrate on a single color for each work. The variations in tones and values are fascinating, sensual and moving. The texture of these works is also a protagonist, without being in any way strident. There is a slight real movement when he uses pieces of leather or mattresses as the ground; or else he achieves an effect of synaesthesia by the way he uses acrylic paint on a conventional canvas.

Another interesting thing about this purification of means of expression is that he produces more and more untitled works. The artist who has so often appropriated literature in his paintings, both explicitly and implicitly, has reached a point at which even the key word of a title is a clue that he no longer needs. All its meaning is contained in his craftsmanship as painter. At times he adopts a distant manner, or else he practices a discourse that is apparently cold and conceptual. Large canvases, traversed only by streets and avenues and painted in a single color; or impersonal maps

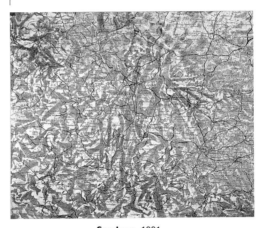

San Juan, 1991
Acrylic on canvas
195 x 170 cm
Collection: Alfonso Pons, Caracas

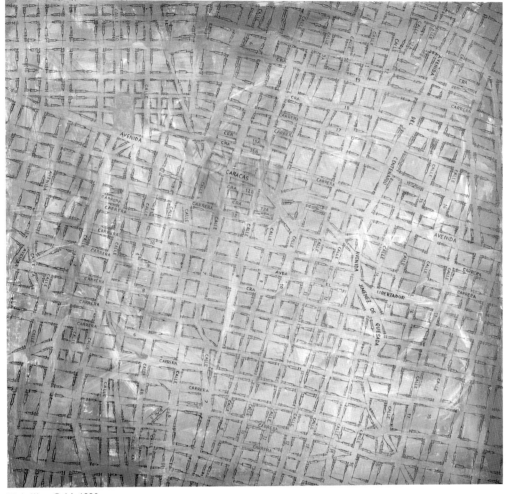

Mainlline Grid, 1990
Acrylic on canvas
200 x 200 cm
Collection: Arthur G. Rosen,
New Jersey
Courtesy: Annina Nosei Gallery
New York

with a metallic glint that freezes the imagery in a style that makes one think of factory-made products. This is the case with works such as *Mainline Grid* (1990), *Cold Steel Streets* (1990) and *San Juan de la Cruz* (1990). Of course this ascetic effect is only one more game in Kuitca's repertoire. On looking closer at his anonymous streets the viewer notices the syringes or swords whose forms are part of this urban grid; their conceptual lines free the image of its apparent coldness.

In the maps of regions, the fanciful and obsessive repetition of the name of a city, in the case of San Juan de la Cruz, opens up another level of meaning: place names are profoundly evocative. Here then it is words that neutralize the apparent depersonalization.

In other maps it is the material painterly intention that dominates the scene. This happens when the cartographic code is transformed into an almost purely artistic game; color and materials, light and lines have the effect of a primordial visual statement. *Untitled roads* (1990) and *Untitled* (1990-91) are obvious examples of this second manner. There is an obvious delight in the painting; the viewer is taken by surprise and surveys with pleasure the surface of these works that has been emphasized in all its materiality. Kuitca has based his imagery on a new balance between concealment and revealing gestures. These two approaches – the conceptual and the material – that we already saw in the maps, is also evident in the series of house plans. *House Plan with Broken Heart* (1990), *Corona de espinas* (1990) and *Bone Built for Eternity* (1990) are typical of this series in which the perimeter of the house plan turns into arteries of the circulation system, into lines made of thorns or constructions of bones. Again the meaning is to be found in the displacement of the ground plan, its metamorphosis into 'talking architecture'.

In *Untitled* (1991) [yellow ground plan] and *Untitled* (1991) [white ground plan on a dark background] the shape of the ground plan is concealed by the visual game by which the texture of a mattress is imitated or else it dissolves in a milky white expanse that makes one think of traces of sperm. The formal structure of the house is transformed into a support for the sensory expanse that is the work of the artist.

Untitled Roads, 1990
Mixed media on mattress
198 x 198 cm
Collection: Gian Enzo Sperone, Rome
Courtesy: Gian Enzo Sperone, Rome

Kuitca: the next stage

Kuitca has succeeded in combining plastic methods, an iconographical discourse and semantics into an original synthesis; he has innovated the basic elements of painting in order to make a personal statement. Theatricality is transformed into poetry; his inventory of objects becomes a single image; fragmentation is transformed into a single center; narrative, into an elementary form.

'I will not make poems with reference to parts, But I will make poems, songs, thoughts with reference to ensemble, And I will not sing with reference to a day but with reference to all days, And I will not make a poem, nor the least part of a poem but has reference to the soul, Because, having looked at the objects of the universe, I find there is no one, nor any particle of one but has reference to the soul.'[10]

200

Notes

1 Jorge Luis Borges: 'Buenos Aires en El Otro, el mismo' (1964) in *Borges Obra poética*, Emecé Editores, Buenos Aires, 1977, p. 273.

2 Nelly Richard: *Latinoamérica y la post-modernidad*, in *Revista de Crítica Cultural*, no. 3, 2nd year, Santiago de Chile, April 1991, p. 15.

3 Nelly Richard, id. p. 19.

4 Martin Rejtman: *Guillermo Kuitca. Mirada interior*, in *Claudia*, November 1992, no. 3, Buenos Aires, p. 68.

5 This list, like all the inventories in this essay, is intended to be informative; it is not exhaustive.

6 'A phenomenon' that obviously has to be understood as occurring in the context of the influence of Latin America on the world, as is confirmed by the position achieved by the younger generation that includes, amongst others, Jac Leirner from Brazil and the Mexican painter, Julio Galán.

7 Article in *Der Spiegel*, Germany, 1979 quoted in *Teatro de Danza de Wuppertal*, programme booklet, Sala Martin Coronado, Teatro General San Martin, season for 1980.

8 Erwin Panofsky: *La perspectiva como forma simbólica*, Tusguets, Barcelona, Second Edition, 1978, p. 10.

9 It is worth remembering that in Freudian theory, shoes are a phallic symbol and that in the world of antiquity footwear was a sign of freedom, because slaves had to walk with bare feet.

10 Walt Whitman: *Starting from Paumanok*, no. 12 in *Leaves of Grass*, The New American Library, New York 1960, p. 45.

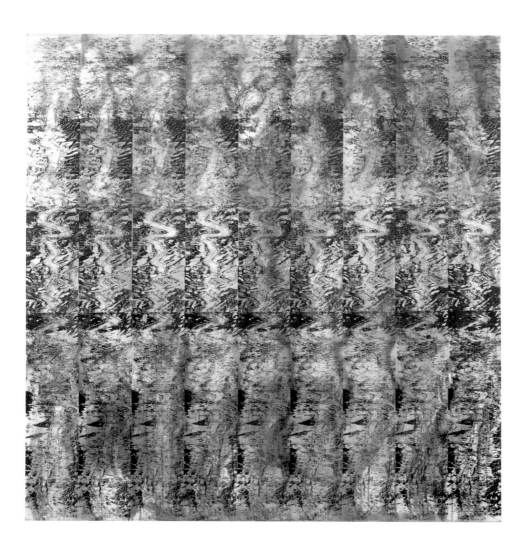

Untitled, 1988
Charcoal on paper
18.7 x 25.8 cm
Collection of the artist

Untitled, 1992
Mixed media on canvas
178 x 168 cm
Courtesy: Sperone Westwater, New
York

Sacramento, 1990
Acrylic on canvas
11 parts
Collection: Mr. and Mrs. Stuart
Kramer, New York
Courtesy: Galerie Barbara Farber,
Amsterdam

Selected Solo Exhibitions

1974
Galeria Lirolay, Buenos Aires
1978
Galeria Christel K., Buenos Aires
1980
Fundación San Telmo, Buenos Aires (catalogue)
1982
CAYC, Centro de Arte y Comunicación, Buenos Aires
1984
Galeria Del Retiro, Buenos Aires (catalogue)
1985
Elisabeth Franck Gallery, Knokke-Le-Zoute (catalogue)
1986
Galeria del Retiro, Buenos Aires
Galeria Thomas Cohn, Rio de Janeiro
1987
Galeria Paulo Figueiredo, São Paulo
1989
Galeria Thomas Cohn, Rio de Janeiro
Galeria Atma, San José, Costa Rica
1990
Annina Nosei Gallery, New York
Kunsthalle Basel, Basel
Galerie Barbara Farber, Amsterdam (catalogue)
Witte de With Center for Contemporary Art, Rotterdam
(catalogue)
Stadtisches Museum, Mulheim
Thomas Solomon's Garage, Los Angeles
Gian Enzo Sperone, Rome (catalogue)
1991
Annina Nosei Gallery, New York (catalogue)
Projects: Guillermo Kuitca, The Museum of Modern Art, New
York (brochure); travelled through 1992: Newport Harbor
Art Museum, Newport Beach (catalogue); The Corcoran
Gallery of Art, Washington; Contemporary Arts Museum,
Houston
Galerie Barbara Farber, Amsterdam
1992
Les Allumées Nantes – Buenos Aires, Chapelle de l'Oratoire –
Musée des Beaux Arts de Nantes, Nantes (brochure)
1993
Guillermo Kuitca, IVAM, Centre del Carme, Valencia (book,
Spanish and English editions); travelling in 1993-1994: Museo
de Monterrey, Monterrey; Museo Rufino Tamayo, Mexico
City; Center for the Fine Arts, Miami; Musée National d'Art
Moderne, Centre G. Pompidou, Paris
Sperone Westwater, New York (catalogue)
Musée d'Art Contemporain de Montréal, Montréal
(brochure)

Selected Group Exhibitions

1980
Premio Braque, Museo de Arte Moderno, Buenos Aires
1981
25 años, Museo de Arte Moderno, Buenos Aires
1982
La Nueva Imagen y 'Pintura Fresca', Galeria del Buen Ayre,
Buenos Aires
Gruppo IIIII, CAYC, Centro de Arte y Comunicación, Buenos
Aires (brochure)
La Anavanguardia, Estudio Giesso, Buenos Aires (catalogue)
Bienal Arche, Museo Nacional de Bellas Artes, Buenos Aires
Premio Braque, Museo Nacional de Bellas Artes, Buenos Aires
1983
Intergrafik '83, Berlin
Artes Visuales y democracia, La Nueva Imagen de los '80s,
CAYC, Centro de Arte y Comunicación, Buenos Aires
Realismo, Tres Vertientes, Museo de América, Madrid; Maison
de l'Amerique Latine, Paris; Moscow and Belgrade
Sieben Maler aus Buenos Aires, DAAD Gallery, Berlin
Buenos Aires a través de sus artistas, Centro Cultural Ciudad
de Buenos Aires, Buenos Aires; Akademie der Kunst, Berlin;
International Union of Architects, XV Congress, Cairo
7 Pintores..., Museo Municipal Bellas Artes Juan B.
Castagnino, Rosario; Museo Provincial de Bellas Artes,
Tucumán (catalogue)
Expresiones '83, Museo de Arte Moderno, Centro Cultural
Ciudad de Buenos Aires (catalogue)
Libros de Artistas, Centro Cultural Ciudad de Buenos Aires
1985
XVIII Bienal de São Paulo, São Paulo (catalogue)
Ideas y imagenes de la Argentina de hoy, Museo de Arte
Moderno, Mexico City; Venezuela, Peru and Brazil
(catalogue)
De Pop Art a la Nueva Imagen, Galeria Ruth Benzacar, Buenos
Aires; Museo Nacional de Artes Plásticas, Montevideo
Instalaciones, Fundación San Telmo, Buenos Aires
Latinoamericanos en Nueva York, M13 Gallery, New York
De la Nueva Figuración a la Nueva Imagen, Museo de Bellas
Artes, Caracas (catalogue)
Soy loco por ti América, Auditorio H. Stern, Rio de Janeiro
1987
Arte Argentino 1810-1987, Instituto Italo-Latinoamericano,
Rome
Art of the Fantastic, Latin America, 1920-1987, Indianapolis
Museum of Art, Indianapolis; The Queens Museum, New
York; Center for the Fine Arts, Miami; Centro Cultural de
Arte Contemporaneo, Mexico City (catalogue)
La Nueva Imagen, dos Generaciones, Galeria Forum, Lima
Argentina, Pintura Joven, Galeria Arte Actual, Santiago
(catalogue)

1988
Salon Internacional Bienal, San José (catalogue)
1989
New Image Painting, Argentina in the Eighties, Americas
Society Art Gallery, New York (catalogue)
U-ABC, Stedelijk Museum, Amsterdam (catalogue); Museum
Calouste Gulbenkian, Lisbon
XX Bienal de São Paulo, São Paulo (catalogue and individual
brochure)
1990
Group Show, Painting, Annina Nosei Gallery, New York
Homage to Van Gogh, Poster Design, Amsterdam (catalogue)
1991
Metropolis, Martin Gropius Bau, Berlin (catalogue)
Personal Portraits, Annina Nosei Gallery, New York
Latin-American Artists, Arnold Herstand Gallery, New York;
Rhode Island School of Design, Providence
Mito y Magia de los '80, Museo de Arte Contemporaneo,
Monterrey (catalogue)
1992
Greg Colson, Guillermo Kuitca, William Wegman, Sperone
Westwater, New York
The Absent Body, Institute of Contemporary Art, Boston
(brochure)
Documenta IX, Kassel (catalogue)
La Colección del IVAM, Instituto Valenciano de Arte Moderno,
Valencia (catalogue)
Artistas Latinoamericanos del Siglo XX, Estación Plaza de
Armas, Seville (catalogue); travelled in 1993: Hotel des Arts,
Paris (catalogue); Kunsthalle, Cologne; The Museum of
Modern Art, New York
1993
Cartographies, Winnipeg Art Gallery, Winnipeg

Books, Catalogues and Other Publications

Monographs

Baechler, Donald. *Guillermo in Rio.* New York: Ajax Press, 1988.

Beeren, Wim, and Lucie-Smith, Edward. *Guillermo Kuitca.* Amsterdam: Galerie Barbara Farber, 1990.

Carvajal, Rina, and Dercon, Chris. *Guillermo Kuitca.* Rotterdam: Witte de With Center for Contemporary Art, 1990.

Driben, Lelia. *Kuitca: XX Bienal de São Paulo.* São Paulo: XX Bienal Internacional de Arte, 1989.

Glusberg, Jorge. *Guillermo Kuitca.* ARCO, Madrid: Galeria del Reitro – Centro de Arte y Comunicación, 1982.

Lebenglik, Fabián. *Guillermo David Kuitca: Obras 1982-1988.* Buenos Aires: Julia Lublin Ediciones, 1988.

Guillermo Kuitca. Nantes: Musée des Beaux Arts, Chapelle de l'Oratoire, CRDC, 1992.

Merewether, Charles. *Guillermo Kuitca.* Rome: Gian Enzo Sperone, 1990.

Oliva, Achille Bonito. *Guillermo Kuitca.* New York: Annina Nosei Gallery, 1991.

Zelevansky, Lynn. *Guillermo Kuitca.* Newport Beach: The Newport Harbor Museum, 1992.

Group Exhibition Catalogues

Artistas Latinoamericanos del Siglo XX. Text by Ed Sullivan. Seville and New York: Ayuntamiento de Sevilla and The Museum of Modern Art, 1992.

Art of the Fantastic. Texts by Rosa Brill, Holliday Day and Hollister Sturges. Indianapolis: Indianapolis Museum of Art, 1987.

Documenta IX. Kassel: Edition Crantz Abrams, 1992.

Homage to Vincent van Gogh. Text by Frits Becht. Amsterdam: Van Gogh Foundation, 1990.

Metropolis. Edited by Christos Joachimides and Norman Rosenthal. Berlin and New York: Martin Gropius Bau and Rizzoli International Publications, 1991.

Mito y Magia en América en los '80s. Text by Francesco Pellizzi. Monterrey: Museo de Arte Contemporáneo, 1991.

New Image Painting, Argentina in the Eighties. Texts by Louis Grachos and Jorge Glusberg. New York: Americas Society, 1989.

XX Bienal Internacional de Arte de São Paulo. São Paulo: Bienal São Paulo, 1989.

XVIII Bienal Internacional de Arte de São Paulo. São Paulo: Bienal São Paulo, 1985.

U-ABC. Texts by Wim Beeren, Dorine Mignot and Guillermo Whitelow. Amsterdam: Stedelijk Museum, 1989.

Selected Articles and Reviews

Alspaugh, Leann Davis. 'Maping Out a Dream, The Art of Guillermo Kuitca.' *Museum & Arts,* Houston (July 1992)

Ayerza, Josefina. 'Guillermo Kuitca at MoMA.' *Flash Art* 24 no161 (November 1991): 129-130.

'Conversation with Guillermo Kuitca.' *Lacanian Ink 1* (1991)

Bolle, Eric. 'Guillermo Kuitca and Julio Galán.' *Metropolis M 4* (September/October 1990)

Borum, Jennifer P. 'Guillermo Kuitca: Annina Nosei Gallery.' *Artforum* 28 no9 (May 1990): 189.

Brenson, Michael. *The New York Times* (9 February 1990)

De Bruyn, Eric. 'Guillermo Kuitca/Julio Galán: Witte de With/Galerie Barbara Farber' *Artscribe* (March/April, 1991): 78-79.

Cantor, Judy. 'Guillermo Kuitca Profile.' *Latin American Art 2* (1991)

'The Wunderkind Painter Turns 27.' *Buenos Aires Herald* (7 February 1988)

Feintuch, Robert. 'Guillermo Kuitca at Annina Nosei.' *Art in America* 78 no9 (September 1990): 198-199.

Gasteiger, A. 'Kuitca.' *Juliet* 38 (October/November 1988): 23.

Glusberg, Jorge. 'International Transavantguard.' *Gian Carlo Politi Editore,* Milan (1983)

Greenless, Donald. 'How to Map the Universe.' *Artnews* 90 no8 (October 1991): 94-95.

Liebman, Lisa. 'Kuitca.' *The New Yorker* 67 no8 (7 October 1991): 13.

Mahoney, Robert. 'New York in Review.' *Arts Magazine* 64 no9 (May 1990): 109.

McCullough, Ed. 'Road Maps of Argentina.' *Beunos Aires Herald* (20 October 1991)

Morsiani, Paola. 'Interview with Guillermo Kuitca.' *Juliet* 48 (June 1990)

Newhall, Edith. 'A Map of the World.' *New York Magazine* 24 no38 (30 September 1991): 72.

Van Nieuwenhuyzen, Martijn. 'Guillermo Kuitca, Julio Galán: Private Apartments, Spanish Pain.' *Flash Art* 23 no55 (November/December 1990): 149.

Pauls, Alan. 'Pequeño Kuitca ilustrado.' BA *Colecciones 1* (1992)

Pellizzi, Francesco. 'Julio Galán.' Witte de With Center for Contemporary Art (1990)

Restany, Pierre. 'La Giovanne Generazione e il Desiderio de Vivere.' *Domus* (Milan) 661 (May 1985): 84-87.

Russell, Taylor John. 'Berlin: The Emperor's New Wardrobe.' *The Times* (26 April 1991)

Shaw, Edward. 'The End of Solitude: Young Artists on the Rise.' *Artnews* 89 no8 (October 1990): 138-143.

Shaw, Edward. 'Guillermo Kuitca: Labour of Love.' *Buenos Aires Herald* (21 July 1991)

Smith, Roberta. 'Guillermo Kuitca.' *The New York Times* (12 April 1990)

Concept
Contemporary Art Foundation
Amsterdam

Text
Carmen Alborch
Eduardo Lipschutz-Villa
Marcelo E. Pacheco
Martin Rejtman
Jerry Saltz

Editor/Coordination
Meghan Ferrill

Translation
Donald Gardner
Edward Shaw

Cover
Eduardo Lipschutz-Villa / Executed by
Hans Bockting and Lex van Pieterson,
based on a painting by Guillermo
Kuitca, *Siete últimas canciones*, 1986
(page 179), configurated in a Barco
Creator at PDI, Amsterdam.

Design
Hans Bockting / Marisa Klaster
(UNA), Amsterdam

Lithography
ColorScan, Loosdrecht

Typesetting and Printing
Lecturis, Eindhoven

Binding
Boekbinderij Van Waarden, Zaandam

Photography

All photograph courtesies are with the respective galleries
and institutes

Victor Arnolds, pp. 115, 148, 185
Alejandro Cherniasky, p. 108 *(Nadie olvida nada)*, 145
(Nadie olvida nada), 179 *(Siete últimas canciones)*, 181 *(Si yo
fuera el invierno mismo)*
Marta Fernandez, p. 108 *(Siete últimas canciones)*
Claudio Gonzales Landa, pp. 10-16, 155, 164-167, 170-
178, 180, 181 *(Sin título; Sin título)*, 188, 191, 194-195
Gustavo Lowry, pp. 113, 145 *(Mi hijo es bello como el sol;
Nadie olvida nada)*, 151, 159 *(People on Fire)*, 186, 200
(Porgy and Bess)
Mariano Molinari, p. 201
Vincenzo Pirozzi, p. 152
Ute Stein, p. 187

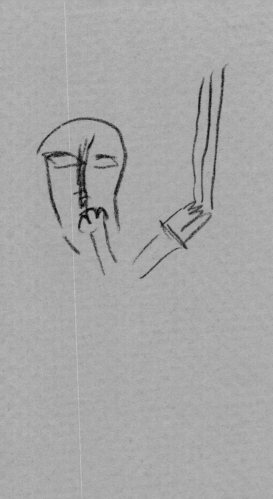